TO THE LEADERS OF OUR WORKING PEOPLE

CLASSICS OF IRISH HISTORY
General Editor: Tom Garvin

Other titles in this series:

TO THE LEADERS
OF OUR
WORKING PEOPLE

Standish James O'Grady

edited by
Edward A. Hagan

University College Dublin Press
Preas Choláiste Ollscoile Bhaile Átha Cliath

This edition first published 2002 by
University College Dublin Press
Introduction, chronology and notes © Edward A. Hagan 2002

ISBN 1 900621 41 x
ISSN 1383–6883

University College Dublin Press
Newman House, 86 St Stephen's Green
Dublin 2, Ireland
www.ucdpress.ie

Cataloguing in Publication data available from the British Library

Typeset in Ireland in Baskerville
by Elaine Shiels, Bantry, Co. Cork
Printed on acid-free paper in Ireland by ColourBooks Ltd, Dublin.

CONTENTS

INTRODUCTION

Edward A. Hagan

The Irish Worker was the weekly newspaper of the Irish labour movement from 1911 until it was suppressed in 1914 when the advent of the First World War made opposition to the war—especially opposition of a Socialist sort—seem seditious to the British government. The newspaper was edited by Jim Larkin, the driving force behind the labour movement, and its circulation was astounding.[1] Larkin's paper pulled no punches and attacked "shameful sweaters, exposing gross inhumanity".[2] Larkin was a staunch Socialist, who viewed the Russian revolution of 1917 with approval and attended the Fifth Congress of the Communist International in Moscow in 1924. Larkin was a militant, confrontational union leader of an almost legendary sort. In 1913 he led the Irish Transport and General Workers Union in many strikes and was eventually opposed by the Employers' Federation led by William Martin Murphy. The strife led to a prolonged lockout and a furious battle with the employers that the union ultimately lost.

Just prior to this most important of early twentieth-century Irish labour battles, Larkin opened the columns, and very often the front page, of *The Irish Worker* to Standish James O'Grady (1846–1928), who wrote long articles for the newspaper from October 1912 through May 1913. Many Irish Studies scholars today, who have trusted W. B. Yeats's rather early and partly incorrect characterization of him in *The Autobiography* as a "hater of every form of democracy",[3] will find this close and comfortable association surprising, even shocking. A view of

O'Grady as the incorrigible, almost archetypal, representative of a decadent Anglo-Irish Ascendancy remains the norm. Yet to W. P. Ryan in 1919, it was obvious that the Irish labour movement was in his debt:

> other distinctive minds that at first had little apparent relation to harassed and militant Labour, were brought [by Larkin and James Connolly] into direct association with it, and gave it ideas that must always be living parts of its gospel. Outstanding examples are "AE " and Pádraic MacPiarais— still earlier Standish O'Grady addressed communal ideas to under-men and world-wasted clerks with something of the glow he had expended a generation before on the coming of Cuchulainn and the fortunes of the Fianna.[4]

Thus *To the Leaders of Our Working People*, a compendium of his *Irish Worker* columns, addresses the need for a revision of contemporary misconceptions of O'Grady. His 1912–13 rhetoric is of a piece with much of his political and social writing for many years prior to that time. There was no miraculous change of mind or heart; O'Grady was always quite unconventional, even inconsistent, in his thinking.

He is usually given credit, as Ryan gives, only for his "bardic histories", published in 1878 and 1880, insofar as they introduced the ancient Irish tales to the writers of the Irish Revival, especially Yeats. In his work after 1908, however, O'Grady, conscious of the possibly damaging value of an invented tradition, tried to persuade Dublin's working class to ignore the Romantic Ireland he had helped to create:

> The necessity of things, your own desperate condition, worsening too, which all the gay causes and movements and the dishonest pseudo-babblings about the glories of ancient Ireland, gods and heroes, and so forth, cannot conceal from you—that fierce Necessity is driving you remorselessly, yet for your good, to combine and associate and go forth out of your house of bondage into the wilderness if necessary

and escape and be free. There is a "Promised Land" before you, too, and flowing with more than "milk and honey," and you need not kill anyone in order to possess it.[5]

Readers of Joyce's *Ulysses* will not find the association of the Irish with the Hebrews unusual, but the passage suggests that O'Grady is far more complicated than the reductive popular view of him; in fact, his work between 1908 and 1913, addressed to Dublin's working class, reveals him as both a practical and visionary advocate of Irish disengagement from a pervasive, totalizing, violent capitalist system. O'Grady, under the strong and acknowledged influence of the Russian anarchist, Prince Peter Alekseyevich Kropotkin, proposed an anarchistic program of commune developments. O'Grady's work appeared in *The Peasant and Irish Ireland* in 1908, in *The Irish Nation and the Peasant* in 1909 and 1910, in *The Irish Review* in 1911 and 1912, in A. R. Orage's progressive *The New Age* in 1913, and in *The Irish Worker* from 1912 to 1913—this last the work here re-published with his later, previously unpublished revisions.[6]

In *The Irish Worker* O'Grady was given considerable space alongside Larkin, Connolly, and the young Sean O'Casey, and display advertisements for the Christmas 1912 number in the weeks leading up to its publication cite O'Grady as its principal attraction. That essay, O'Grady's "On Heroes and the Heroic: An Address to Young Ireland", occupied the entire first two pages of the Christmas number. It is a kind of Hegelian retrospective on Irish history, i.e., an exposition of the variances in *Zeitgeist* that produced different ascendancies: the ancient heroes, the hero-saints of Christianity, the Anglo-Irish aristocracy, and the peasant of O'Grady's day. O'Grady clearly had established bona fides as a voice that could lend great moral and political weight to working-class movements such as Larkin's labour union.

Understanding the late O'Grady offers the possibility of broadening our understanding of what Yeats meant when he said in "Coole Park and Ballylee":

We were the last romantics—chose for theme
Traditional sanctity and loveliness;
Whatever's written in what poets name
The book of the people; whatever most can bless
The mind of man or elevate a rhyme;

For O'Grady's late "book of the people" is of a piece with his Romantic forebears and with his own early enthusiasm for both Thomas Carlyle and Walt Whitman. Too often scholars ignore O'Grady's oft-stated enthusiasm for Whitman, just as the resemblance of the Whitman of *Democratic Vistas* to Carlyle's spiritual ideals is not easily grasped or remembered. O'Grady saw well the movements of Spirit that were to overtake his decadent class; finally he embraced the lower classes of Dublin—at least for a time.

Accordingly it is possible to open our way into seeing how Ireland participated in twentieth-century European movements of thought and politics, especially evident in the nature of the contending forces in the Spanish Civil War. Like fascists throughout Europe, O'Grady entertains the kind of fascination with Spirit that led to the ascents to power of Mussolini and Hitler and is manifested in the films of Leni Riefenstahl and Sergei Eisenstein. On the other hand, he views mass movements such as those films depict with great alarm. Thus his solution calls for a kind of Romantic boycott of civilization. Above all, he believes that the greatest danger to the Irish labour movement is its co-optation into the façade of liberal democracy that disguises the state violence of capitalism. Against the military power of the Demon State, the workers, in O'Grady's view, were powerless. Socialism and Syndicalism, he argued, were wonderful systems, but since they involved mass movements and confrontations with the State, the results would be disastrous. He believed that State Socialism was cast in the same power terms as capitalism. His view of freedom involves escape from State politics: the examples of lack of freedom are England and America: "you have England and America to teach you—that political freedom is not freedom at all, but a change of tyrants, and generally, a change for the worse" (p. 95 below).

O'Grady's late works reveal a staunch anti-capitalist, a thoroughgoing anarchist who has little belief in constitutional or administrative solutions to Ireland's problems, still less in the "direct action" espoused by syndicalists against capitalist owners of the means of production. O'Grady believed in an imaginative, essential human nature that constitutions and administrations only had talent for thwarting. He believed that a human, unfettered by capitalism, is idealistic—"a being who naturally delights in every kind of creative activity" (p. 29 below). And O'Grady perceived the jeopardy in modern, capitalist society of his view of the human. From 1908 to 1910, he addressed his scheme for rural communes to what he saw as a class of celibate, indentured slaves, Dublin's clerks, created by capitalist economics. Dublin was a fetid, unhealthy mess that served the employers well by harbouring a desperate, surplus labour supply, utterly bereft of the natural creative spirit. In the country he saw the dominance of strong farmers who were squeezing out competition. Indeed in 1908 he attacked a Jesuit leader of the Co-operative movement, Father Thomas Finlay, for accepting the capitalist definition of the human. Father Finley, "who in the Spring of this year, was not ashamed!—to appear in public before the men of Ireland! and declare that no one could be expected to do any kind of work without the incentive of gain."[7] O'Grady speaks in similar Romantic terms in *The Irish Worker* in 1913 when he argues that Christianity has been compromised:

> Hence, in all countries, where civilization holds sway the working people, feeling profoundly that the religions, as practised, are against them, and on the side of their exploiters, are growing neglectful of religion altogether. The British working man does not go to church on Sundays. Generally, I believe, he lies in bed taking a good rest, and reading his favourite sporting paper. (p. 80 below).

O'Grady seems to have understood that in the twentieth century the "élan, enthusiasm and gladness" that communal work and religious worship should produce is now accessible only "in connection with athletics or sport".[8] He, like many nineteenth-century Protestant church historians and sages such as Coleridge and Arnold, viewed the church as a progressive development of an increasingly secular, national, non-dogmatic idea of religion. Indeed Coleridge used a term, "the clerisy"[9] to broaden the idea of the clergy to include other secular kinds of leaders. He used this term in *On the Constitution of Church and State*, where he also argued that Church and State evolved as manifestations of what Hegel called Spirit. Thus, "History studied in the light of philosophy . . . [is] the great drama of an ever unfolding Providence".[10] As Arnold was concerned about fracturing the national polity by allowing religious fragmentation to create "*hole-and-corner* forms of religion",[11] O'Grady also sought to create a broad religious pluralism that would allow for a certain range of Christian sects, but not "*hole-and-corner*" sports, a kind of opium of the masses. He worried about the hostilities that could arise from one locality to another over the exact nature of God or the winner of the local hurling match. Thus he argued for a decentralized system of small communes that would each have its own gods (somewhat like some Native American tribes). And, though O'Grady wants "a revolution of which Christ would approve, and over which the angels will rejoice" (p. 80 below), his view of Christianity is also tinged with scepticism, for it "strikes a certain chill—seems to darken the scene perceptibly, as if a cloud crossed the sun".[12] Indeed, in line with Coleridge's idea of the evolving nature of "Church", he says, "I submit that going to a picnic, or into any kind of society animated by the same spirit is perhaps a[s] religious a practice as going to church."[13]

O'Grady studied Classics at Trinity College, Dublin, in the 1860s and was a lifelong student of ancient Greek societies, particularly those he believed were "animated by the same spirit". He uses Greek models, particularly Sparta (as did fascists), almost exclusively in his later work[14] and seems mostly to have dismissed his Romantic notions of Cuculain.[15] (He preferred Sparta to Athens because of the latter's alleged anti-proletarian values: "slaves [in Athens] outnumbered the freemen by ten to one".[16]) He speaks with great certainty about the nature of Spartan village life and argues that city-states were limited by Spartan rules to groups of 300 self-sufficient people: "A beautiful example of such natural prim-itive instinctive socialism is supplied by the little independent communal or semi-communal States of ancient Greece— friendly, independent States with territories often as small as the areas of our own parishes!" (p. 32 below). He argues that "Ireland will yet be a Commonwealth of Commonwealths; a Nation of many nations, and every Nation a Commune" (p. 46 below).

That ideal contrasts with the conventional political idea of "nation" and makes O'Grady a fellow traveller with many contemporary postcolonial critics of Irish history. He points to England as the example of what Ireland does not want to become:

> England is a nation. What are all such nations or that of which you dream you[r] foolish dreams, but hideous exaggerations of the enslaved, held together by a common terras, a common ground, and—ball cartridges.[17]

Indeed O'Grady seems to fear that capitalist forces already have made it impossible for the concept of Nation to be other than the British model:

> The Irish Nation dreamed of so vainly and so tragically by generations of Irishmen would be no true nation. It would be what all nations are to-day, an accumulation of great numbers of different kinds of people with a multitude of separate selfish and conflicting interests, all held together by armed force, that armed force under the control and direction of the most powerful and well disciplined classes

and interests. Such an Ireland would not be a Nation. It would be more properly an Empire . . .[18]

O'Grady's concern may also reflect the tension between the nationalists and the labour union proponents, who often viewed themselves as part of the international Socialist movement. Larkin actively enlisted the support of British labour unions for his strikes, and syndicalist strategy often involved deliberate ignoring of national boundaries. At the time of O'Grady's writing in *The Irish Worker*, Sean O'Casey was also a frequent contributor to the newspaper. O'Casey's columns reflect the tension between the labour movement's Irish Citizen Army and the nationalist Irish Volunteers—both organizations designed to use physical force to protect and promote their interests. O'Grady saw such physical force movements as futile and therefore saw an anarchistic co-operative society as the mode of human re-organization most likely to escape capitalist hegemony, for he well understood the military power of capitalist states. In *Ireland after History*, David Lloyd argues that:

> the phenomenon of violence must be understood as constitutive of social relations within the colonial capitalist state, whose practices institutionalize a violence which, though cumulative, daily and generally unspectacular, is normalized precisely by its long duration and chronic nature.[19]

O'Grady's writing is full of just this point; it represents the logic behind his "drop out" anarchism. While some of O'Grady's rhetoric could earn him the label Hegelian—and therefore to some—a fascist intent on creating the absolute spirit that coalesces a nation into an absolute State, O'Grady's intense consciousness of what Lloyd describes led him in the opposite direction. Indeed Lloyd's book and O'Grady's late work, though separated by some 80 to 90 years, make remarkably similar critiques of Ireland under capitalism. In his writings to working-class Dublin clerks in *The Peasant* and *The Irish Nation* between 1908 and 1910, O'Grady's particular "spin" on

Sinn Féin, for example, was to emphasize its democratic nature in so far as the strong leaders favoured by fascism could no longer be trusted. In 1908 he writes: "Trust your own selves. Sinn Féin!"[20] He urges the use of the Sinn Féin bank, and is sharply critical of "Press, Pulpit and Platform". He counsels the clerks to "take a leaf out of the book of the Sinn Feiners and, trust in no one only in your own selves".[21] The times called for a Whitmanesque greatness in each working man and woman that could be developed in the unstructured world of the commune where "The one grand rule for all will be Freedom!—personal and communal."[22] Throughout all of these writings and in *To the Leaders of Our Working People*, however, O'Grady does offer detailed, meticulous, practical advice about how to make a commune possible: he discusses the type of land needed, its cost, the need for sound agricultural advice from Horace Plunkett's Irish Agricultural Organisation Society, the kind of accommodations necessary at the start, and even the need not to "be afraid of a glass or two extra"[23] on special occasions.

His practicality, however, does not stop O'Grady from using a Hegelian paradigm for his thinking about anarchism; he proclaims: "I am out for the making of Nations [note the plural] and the revolutionizing of Ireland, the reassertion of the eternal laws in temporary things, of divine law in human affairs."[24] In making this manifesto, O'Grady aligns himself with the Hegel of *The History of Philosophy* which declares "that the unity of the divine and human nature should come to the consciousness of man, and that, indeed, on the one hand as an implicitly existent unity, and, on the other, in actuality as worship . . . Not external nature alone, but the whole world pertains to the particular; above all must human individuality know itself in God."[25]

In 1913 O'Grady likens human life to the life of bees and sees a Romantic wholeness to existence that Hegel would approve:

> When the bee population becomes excessive, when there is not honey enough for all, the bees, with a wisdom greater than ours and a fine spirit of adventure, hope and faith,

conceive and accomplish a grand exodus or trek around
their queen, led, one might almost think, by God himself;
surely inspired, guided by a guardian spirit, deriving its
wisdom from the infinite wisdom which made and upholds
all things. They go out into the unknown, nothing doubting
(p. 96 below).

That idea of the Trek becomes O'Grady's mantra in *To the
Leaders of Our Working People*: in view of the overcrowding of
Dublin's working class into hovels, he devised a scheme for
the workers to organize a return to the country where
O'Grady saw relief from air and water pollution as well as the
opportunity to create the wealth of farm produce, but not
capital. Self-sustenance would be the only goal. The initial
"settlers" would be supported by the contributions of the
working class back in the city (and not by emigrants to
America), who would have more space with the settlers'
hovels in Dublin vacated. And then like the bees, new Treks
would multiply the number of communes. Most importantly,
all of this could be accomplished without alarming the state's
ability to make violence. Moreover O'Grady has devised a
system of relief for the urban congestion of Dublin not contin-
gent on emigration. He is keenly conscious of land exploitation
and ruination as the result of making capitalist manipulation
of the economy seem rational and natural. He specifically
takes a shot at Lord Iveagh, the Guinness robber-baron (whose
workers Larkin failed to organize because they were the best
paid in Dublin), for turning Irish wealth into money and taking
it to England.

His strong anti-capitalism grows out of what he sees as its
fake benign nature: "Money is not what they pretend it to
be—'an innocent medium of exchange.' It is Power." The
only way out for the working classes is to recognize that
"though it is hard to make money, and for working people
impossible, it is easy to create every kind of wealth" (p. 83
below). O'Grady therefore opposed the transfer of land from
tillage to cattle raising and argued that advanced methods of

tillage could support Dublin's burgeoning population without emigration.

That population, however, to see an alternative to capitalist "rationalization" of agriculture and emigration, needed a different kind of education. O'Grady saw education as socialization into capitalism and a satanic deadening of consciousness by irrelevant "training": "the Prince of Power of this world at last succeeded in getting me indoors to a desk, and made me learn, amongst other twaddle, the boundaries of the various German States, Mecklenberg-Schwertz and so forth."[26] In its place O'Grady supported technical education much as T. H. Huxley had done in England. O'Grady probably came to these ideas via Kropotkin who advocated a practical outdoor education in which children would learn by doing first hand. O'Grady, a prolific journalist, was not even convinced of the value of literacy as he saw it as a capitalist tool for the enslavement of children in their eventual employment as clerks. He was particularly sceptical of the value of the language revival movement, arguing first in a kind of proto-Montessori vein that "no boy is to be whipped into language-study or into anything else against which his being revolts".[27] But a certain hard-headed pragmatism scorns a mystical view of Irish:

> "Language!" A man can be a scoundrel as effectually with Gaelic words in his false mouth as with Saxon. What has language for the mother who was shrieking this morning in Glasnevin, and who is starving and drinking to-night in a slum?[28]

In the same Christmas 1912 issue of *The Irish Worker* that leads with O'Grady, Maud Gonne strongly criticizes the National Schools as death-traps for children in which the "children are taught to forget the high deeds of our ancestors, the language they spoke and the songs of their poets, and they are taught also to forget the beauty and the sacredness of the land, the beauty of the mountains, the lakes and the rivers, the sweetness of the growing grasses and of the flowers."

Gonne goes on to call the National Schools "the anti-chambers of the lunatic asylums and the workhouse; . . . the foundation stones of tuberculosis sanatoriums; . . . sombre factories for the destruction of our race."[29] In this context O'Grady's endorsement, repeated in *To the Leaders of Our Working People*, of outdoor child labour in an anarchistic society actually seems like a necessary defence against capitalist exploitation.

Thus in O'Grady's view, capitalism institutionalizes its devices for subjugating the masses; in fact, "Universities are amongst the chief agencies by which the brute god, Mammon, holds men in subjection. All their pretensions to the contrary notwithstanding, they enslave the soul, and keep it enslaved, as the Press does and as Religions do."[30] His thinking resembles James Connolly's with the major exception that O'Grady believed that the working class would be slaughtered in open battle. He believed in avoiding violence; thus his anarchism was a kind of "dropping out" of the mainstream. Connolly resembles O'Grady in so far as he sees the workers as enslaved by capital and believes firmly in the necessity of spiritual regeneration of the Irish workers. His assessment is that the conditions exist for revolution, but the people are unaware of their own condition. He writes in that same Christmas 1912 number of *The Irish Worker*:

> Considering the state of slavery in which the masses of the Irish workers are to-day, . . . a state of restlessness, of "divine discontent," on the part of Labour in Ireland is an absolutely essential pre-requisite for the realisation of any spiritual uplifting of the nation at large. With a people degraded, and so degraded as to be unconscious of their degradation, no upward march of Ireland is possible . . .[31]

But Connolly goes on to distinguish his position from O'Grady's: he argues that

> a victory of any kind for the Working Class is better for the cause, more potent for Ultimate Victory than a correct

understanding of Economic Theory by a beaten Labour
Army. The Modern Labour Movement is suspicious of
theorizing that shirks conflict . . . every time the labourer,
be it man or woman, secures triumph in the battle for juster
conditions, the mind of the labourer receives that impulse
towards higher things that comes from the knowledge of
power. . . . the victories of the organised Working Class are
as capable of being stated in terms of spiritual uplifting as
in the material terms of cash.[32]

Connolly's position that the Irish needed "spiritual uplifting"
is consistent with O'Grady's view, but Connolly sought violent
confrontation, undeterred by the impossibility of its success.

Given O'Grady's latter-day association with Connolly,
Gonne, and Larkin, it may seem logical to those accustomed
to associating O'Grady with conservatism to wonder what
tree he was standing under when the lightning struck. But his
later ideas do not depart inexplicably from his earlier ideas.
Described as a "Fenian Unionist" by Lady Gregory, he berated
the Ascendancy class throughout his life; he re-published
Shelley's *Necessity of Atheism* during his Trinity College days;
and in 1875 in *The Gentleman's Magazine* he published the first
article praising Walt Whitman to appear in a European
journal. While it is true that some of the statements in his
early work might fairly be characterized as "Conservative and
Imperialist",[33] as John Kelly and Eric Domville do in their
edition of Yeats's letters from 1865 to 1895, there is real danger
of distortion by reduction when their authority is accepted
uncritically. After 1900, in addition to Kropotkin, he acknowledged the influence of Charles Fourier (Brook Farm was a
Fourier commune) and Henry George (*Progress and Poverty*), and,
at times, he quoted Ruskin's *Fors Clavigera* although he did
regard it as lower-class advocacy written for the upper classes.

To trace the influences upon O'Grady is to undo his work
somewhat because influence implies that history has a con-
nectedness and wholeness such as Hegel would value, that the
process of bringing historical movements to consciousness is

progress towards the absolute. However, while O'Grady may be usefully compared to Hegel, his anarchism resists totalising and makes him our contemporary in seeing history as the work of blinding consciousness to injustice, that, for example,

> the great age of the Greeks was pre-historic, that the Greeks, in respect to their women, as well as their own men, began to fail and fade as they emerged into what we call History.
>
> And this is exactly what we ought to expect, for History, the poor snob, follows almost eloquently and admiringly in the track of strong crime, of successful rapine, of tyranny and slavery, of slaughter on a grand scale, and is, perhaps necessarily, dumb concerning the ages of virtue and innocence and simple piety and goodness and kindly friendly inter-tribal relations, those of clan with clan, village with village, deme with deme.[34]

In that light O'Grady's commune project is an attempt to drop out of history, to create the local virtue that exists outside history's tyranny.

                    *   *   *

Despite the apparent radicalism of O'Grady's anarchism, a sceptical view of *To the Leaders of Our Working People* might suggest that he was desperately trying to find a way out for his class as he saw the coming violence of 1916 and, later, the Irish Civil War. This view cannot be discounted entirely as the few available facts about his later career suggest that he was a supporter of Britain in the First World War, and his son, Standish Conn, was an ace in the Royal Flying Corps. O'Grady himself moved out of Ireland *c.*1918, perhaps in fear of reprisals from revolutionaries who had no time for his attempts to conciliate the rift that led to partition. In a series of articles in the American newspaper, *The Christian Science Monitor*, in 1918,[35] O'Grady promoted views of Irish history consistent with the views of his class; he would have won few friends for his trouble among the newly ascendant bourgeois elite. And Jim Larkin was to discover a few years later how few his friends were when his union was taken over by leaders like Thomas Foran and William O'Brien who were more acceptable to that elite.

But *To the Leaders of Our Working People* can also be seen as a way of returning Ireland to the feudalism that lingered rather late in Ireland, eliminated finally by the Great Hunger as well as by the growth of capitalism that was transforming the country's agriculture from tillage to cattle raising. O'Grady's communes, especially as conceived in the comparison with bees, would set up the kind of decentralized society out of which an aristocracy would naturally spring. It is not hard to imagine that O'Grady would then have created a role in society for the members of his class not rendered thoroughly decadent by the dissolute behaviour characteristic of too many of them in O'Grady's view.

However, it would probably be going too far to accuse O'Grady of subterfuge in the promotion of his commune scheme. Ever the idealist, he would not easily imagine the suspicion that a man of his class could inspire simply by the nature of his discourse. It is a fact, however, that, while he was a journalist for most of his life and thus never sounds like an out-of-touch intellectual, *To the Leaders of Our Working People* is written most curiously. It alludes frequently to the King James Version of the Bible and even to Article 31 of the 39 Articles of the Church of England. Article 31's condemnation of the Catholic Mass makes his allusion seem hardly politic. Since he was the son and brother of Church of Ireland ministers and the father of a Church of England minister and was once a divinity student himself at Trinity, there is no surprise in his very strong command of the King James Version. It is probably unlikely that he would think that the predominantly Catholic readership of *The Irish Worker* would take offence although the pervasive nature of the allusions would sound like that of the local parson to Catholic ears. Although his discourse presents a difficult critical problem, a plausible explanation lies in his desire to restore Ireland to the kind of society that he believed the Bible actually envisions. In testifying to its impact on him personally through its support for his view of ideal Irish "Nations", O'Grady is most "Protestant" in the individuality of his faith. O'Grady's antagonism to institutional authority and his conscious recreation of the prehistoric Spirit fits with his sense of the Bible as a spiritual book. Like some other writers, he believed Ireland had too much religion and not enough Spirit.

NOTES

1   "In its first month, June, 1911, the circulation figure was 26,000. In July it was 64,500, in August, 74,750, and in September, 94,994. From this peak month it levelled off to something over 20,000 a week". Emmet Larkin, *James Larkin: Irish Labour Leader, 1876–1947* (Cambridge, MA: MIT Press, 1965), p. 78. In *The Irish Labour Movement* (Dublin: Talbot; London: T. Fisher Unwin, 1919), p. 197, W. P. Ryan writes: "For Irish weekly proletarian or democratic journalism the circulation was astonishing; and it might have been much greater; the modest machinery was unable to meet the demand."

2   Ryan, *Labour Movement*, p. 197.

3   W. B. Yeats, *The Autobiography of W.B. Yeats* (New York: Collier Books, 1974), 148.

4   Ryan, *Irish Labour Movement*, p. 11.

5   Standish James O'Grady, "Consider the Lilies", in *Render to Caesar: The Social Problem From An Irish Point Of View*, The Standish DeCourcey O'Grady Collection, p. 92. (*Render to Caesar* is an unpublished, edited and revised (by O'Grady), book-length compilation of O'Grady's columns originally published in *The Peasant* and *The Irish Nation* from 1908 to 1910 when Ryan edited these newspapers.)

6   It appears that O'Grady intended to publish much of this work in book form as he had previously followed up serialization with book publication. His editing work seems to have been done in 1914 or after. O'Grady was a journalist for most of his career, so he was accustomed to voluminous and not closely edited writing—thus the need for later refinement.

7   Standish James O'Grady, "Turn & Fight Them" in *Render to Caesar*, p. 60. O'Grady's attack resembles Joyce's depiction of the Jesuit preacher in "Grace"—written in 1905, but not published until 1914. Both Joyce and O'Grady were well aware of a comfortable relationship between the Roman Catholic Church and capitalism.

8   "The Dagda's Cauldron", in *Render to Caesar*, p. 82.

9   Samuel Taylor Coleridge, *On the Constitution of Church and State* (1830; rpt., *The Collected Works of Samuel Taylor Coleridge*, vol. 10, Ed. John Colmer, Princeton: Princeton University Press, 1976), p. 46.

10   Coleridge, *Constitution of Church and State*, p. 32.

11   Matthew Arnold, *Culture and Anarchy* (London: Cambridge University Press, 1971), p. 16.

12   "A Pleasant Picnic", in *Render to Caesar*, p. 84.

13   "Picnic", in *Render to Caesar*, p. 83.

14   The title of his 1912 article in *The Irish Review*, "Paganism—Greek and Irish", suggests this penchant.

15   O'Grady's spelling of Cuculain is used throughout.

16   "In the Sweat", in *Render to Caesar*, p. 40.

17   "Vista!", in *Render to Caesar*, p. 68.

18   "The Making of Nations", in *Render to Caesar*, p. 133.

19   David Lloyd, *Ireland after History* (Notre Dame, IN: University of Notre Dame Press, 1999), pp. 3–4.

20   "Melancholy to the Deuce", in *Render to Caesar*, p. 54.

21   "The Downrushing of Rural Ireland", in *Render to Caesar*, p. 49.

22   "Consider the Lilies" in *Render to Caesar*, p. 94.

23   "The Way Home", in *Render to Caesar*, pp. 75–6.

24   "Vista!", in *Render to Caesar*, p. 68.

25   G. W. F. Hegel, *Hegel's Lectures on the History of Philosophy*, Tr. E. S. Haldane and Frances H. Simson (London: Routledge & Kegan Paul, 1896), vol. III, pp. 2–3.

26   "Initial Steps", in *Render to Caesar*, p. 52.

27   "Practical Suggestions", in *Render to Caesar*, p. 67.

28   "Vista!", in *Render to Caesar*, p. 68.

29   Maud Gonne, "Our Irish Children", *The Irish Worker*, Christmas 1912, p. 32, cols. 2–3.

30   "Blind Alleys & Deceiving Cries", in *Render to Caesar*, 87.

31   James Connolly, "Some Rambling Remarks", *The Irish Worker*, Christmas 1912, p. 4, col. 2.

32   *Ibid.*, p. 4, col. 3.

33   John Kelly and Eric Domville, "Biographical and Historical Appendix", in W.B. Yeats, *The Collected Letters of W.B. Yeats* (Oxford: Clarendon; New York: Oxford University Press, 1986), vol. I, p. 502. Kelly and Domville's biographical sketch (pp. 501–3) of O'Grady and their notes on his works reflect solid scholarship, but the sketch makes no mention of his works after 1907, which might have caused them to reconsider their characterization of him.

34   Standish James O'Grady, "Greek Women", in *Air and Wind*, TS, The Standish DeCourcey O'Grady Collection, pp. 6–7.

35   In the second article in the "British Record in Ireland Examined" series, which appeared on 16 September 1918, in the *Christian Science Monitor*, O'Grady must have aroused nationalist ire by saying: "If the strong hand of a lawful and long-established authority were to be removed tomorrow we would not need eight years to reduce the country to desert. There would not be many of us [perhaps narrowly intended, i.e., the Anglo-Irish upper class] left after eight months of it. Our rebels and revolutionaries, fed upon patriotic poetry and rhetoric, with their innocent shouting of 'Ireland a Nation,' and 'Down with England,' 'Down with Dublin Castle,' have no understanding at all of the social hell from which they are continually preserved by that same much abused Dublin Castle with its power of intervention in crises and its immense prestige extending down unbroken for more than seven centuries." 8, col. 1.

STANDISH JAMES O'GRADY:
A CHRONOLOGY

1846 Born to Thomas and Susanna O'Grady. Thomas O'Grady was the Church of Ireland Rector of Castletown Berehaven in County Cork.

1864 Begins as a divinity student at Trinity College, Dublin, but soon turns to the classics and law.

1872 Called to the Bar.

c.1873 Begins his career as leading-article writer for the unionist Dublin *Daily Express*.

1875 Republishes Shelley's tract in support of atheism; publishes the first positive article on Walt Whitman to appear in a major European journal, *The Gentleman's Magazine*.

1878 *History of Ireland: The Heroic Period*.

1880 *History of Ireland: Cuculain and His Contemporaries*, his so-called "bardic histories"—credited with being a seminal influence on the writers of the Irish Renaissance.

1882 *The Crisis in Ireland*. An address to the landlords of Ireland calling them to attend to their duties.

1886 *Toryism and the Tory Democracy*. A political tract dedicated to Lord Randolph Churchill and his "Tory Democracy" ploy to broaden the Tory electoral base.

1889 *Red Hugh's Captivity*. The first of several historical fictions about Elizabethan Ireland.

1894 *The Story of Ireland*. A short, selective Irish history, later regretted but written in a fit of pique with Irish Nationalists.

1895   *The Chain of Gold*—his most famous of several novels for boys, apparently his only book ever to return a profit.

1897   *The Flight of the Eagle*. The most well known of his Elizabethan books.

1898   *All Ireland*, a political tract advocating redress for the over taxation of Ireland during much of the nineteenth century—a cause which he believed all Irish men and women could agree to promote.

     Leaves the *Daily Express*; moves to Kilkenny where he edits *The Kilkenny Moderator* until 1900 when a disastrous libel suit forces him to give up the newspaper.

1900   *The Queen of the World*—a science fiction utopian novel published under the pseudonym, Luke Netterville.

1900–7   edits and publishes *All Ireland Review*, a weekly newspaper designed to promote the commonweal of all segments of Irish society.

1907   *The Masque of Finn*, a play later performed by the boys at St. Enda's, Padraic Pearse's school.

1908–10   writes lengthy serialized columns, advocating Fourier-style "communism" for W. P. Ryan's newspapers, *The Peasant and Irish Ireland* and *The Irish Nation and the Peasant*.

1912–13   *The Irish Worker* columns.

1913   publishes an article in A.R. Orage's *The New Age*, a journal which promotes "guild socialism".

1913–14   visits America as the guest of John Quinn, the collector of modernist manuscripts and artwork.

1914–18   Son, Standish Conn, is an ace in the Royal Flying Corps during the First World War

1917   *The Departure of Dermot*. A short account, full of adulation for the King who first brought the English to Ireland, but also respect for the manner of his departure from Ireland.

1918   Publishes a sceptical view of Irish nationalism in the American *Christian Science Monitor*. Tries to heal the

breach with N.E. Ulster by proposing that a Protestant
lead an initial Home Rule government.

1920   *The Triumph and Passing of Cuculain.*
1928   Dies, in retirement on the Isle of Wight.

NOTE ON THE TEXT

To the Leaders of Our Working People and other contributions by O'Grady were published in *The Irish Worker* from 12 October 1912 to 10 May 1913. O'Grady apparently intended to compile all of *The Irish Worker* columns into a single volume and publish it as a book. A newspaper writer for most of his adult life, O'Grady commonly serialized his essays and some novels in newspapers and later compiled them for publication as books.

O'Grady did indeed revise the columns that appeared from 12 October 1912 through 30 November 1912, apparently with a book in mind. Thus the first part of the text published here presents the revised, previously unpublished edition of those early columns. O'Grady's grandson, Standish DeCourcey O'Grady, preserved this edited version. The revision cuts substantial parts of the columns as published in *The Irish Worker*. The cuts have been restored here with notes indicating where O'Grady cut the originally published version. Notes also indicate other significant wording changes in the revised edition. The dates of original publication in *The Irish Worker* appear in square brackets in the revised portion of the text.

TO THE LEADERS OF OUR WORKING PEOPLE.

[*The Irish Worker*, 12 October 1912]

You are beginning to think, I perceive, that, some time through the power of organized Labour, you may become the governing authority of this island and assume the direction of its destinies.

It is a great ambition, a grand objective, one, too, which is perfectly realizable if you on your side will but think and act in a spirit commensurate with the greatness of the position to which you aspire. In this land power which was once wielded by kings, chieftains, earls, passed from them to landlords, and, in our time, seems to be trending in your direction, also will arrive if you on your side do not make mistakes.

Even to-day, through the workmen and labourers of village, town and country, you appear to possess a preponderance of political power if only you can rightly bring it into action, and an immense preponderance of physical force, always a source of incalculable strength whether voteless or voting.

Add now to this, your decided superiority, some four hundred thousand small farmers, men who till their ground with their own hands, who therefore are essentially workmen and labourers like yourselves, they and their sons a vital portion of the great army of Labour. They are men whom you might easily antagonize by a too exclusive policy as you antagonized them in the last great railway strike[1] when you would not convey their goods to market.

Add now the many thousands of clerks and shop assistants in or out of employment—perhaps 50,000 of them all Ireland over—they are part of your vast unorganised army of labour.

Add again the certainty of the political enfranchisement of women which will double our political power.

Add, too, a proportion of those whom, for convenience sake, we may call the classes, and all who born in any class represent the mind, conscience and imagination of our country, and who regard with aversion the tendency of the times towards the commercialization of all things, the advance of the money power to universal dominion. Finally, I think the secret sympathies of all the clergymen of all the religions are with you. How can we think otherwise, remembering whose servants and ministers they profess themselves to be? Their present dependence upon Mammon has been forced upon them. Free them and they will be yours. To-day they are unable to speak what is in their hearts. Did you ever hear a sermon on "the Sermon on the Mount", or an intelligent explanation of that deep saying about the Camel and the Needle's Eye?[2] I never did.

All these orders are your natural allies. Beware of antagonizing or alienating any of them.

You possess both patent and latent a vast, an overwhelming power which nevertheless you cannot use, and it is the same everywhere. In all civilized lands we see the workers of the world possessed of a mighty power which they are unable to bring into action. In the hands of the propertied exploiting and ruling classes you are as powerless as a sparrow in the claws of a hawk. The creators and maintainers of the wealth of the world possess, too, the power to govern the world and direct the distribution of the world's wealth, but won't or can't.

Why?

What is it that holds such millions of brave, strong, intelligent men in a condition of virtual slavery? You know yourselves that Irish self-government won't end here a condition so universal and proceeding evidently from some deep cause. Here, as elsewhere, property will rule you, and, if you rebel, shoot you.

You think now, I know, of bigger strikes, national strikes, international strikes, of more desperate efforts to get your men into Parliament, of, so, capturing the State and using its powers and resources for the solution of the sore problems that beset labour.

You can't do such things. The power of Capitalism is too great for you, too disciplined and intelligent; though you may

very well in the attempt precipitate the Social Revolution. But
that is a counsel of despair. Few of us would survive to tell
what a Social Revolution is like.

I believe you understand yourselves the reasons why you
cannot lift up and carry forward the masses of the people by
the strike method. Your failure in politics in your efforts to
seize the State and wield its resources arises from a kindred
cause, the inherent weakness of mere sensitive shrinking flesh
and blood pitting itself against a thing so devoid of bowels as
money, and therefore possessed of such staying power, and
many other kinds of power, too. You can see everywhere—it
is evident fact—that political power follows property, and that
the impropertied, those whose means of existence from week
to week are in the hands of others, are out of that game. All
this, the futility of strikes, the futility of politics, apparent long
since to attentive observers, has been of late lucidly and con-
vincingly explained by the Editor[3] of "The New Age", who in
consequence, has decided in favour of Syndicalism.[4]

What is Syndicalism? Doubtless, you know yourselves all
about it, it being your business, your interest and duty to
understand, this proposed third way of escape. But as others
beside you will read this, many of them young people thinking
about things for the first time, I shall write a few sentences
concerning this new method of Syndicalism, whose advocates
believe in it so profoundly and are now preaching it with such
zeal. The thoughts of the younger, bolder, and more imaginative
of labour leaders in England are certainly tending thitherward.[5]

Syndicalism means the seizure of the means and implements of
production—the railways by the railway men, the mines by the miners,
wharves by the dockers, ships by the sailors, factories by the hands, and
so on. This course is being now pressed upon you by very clever men in
these islands and on the Continent, and it is quite possible that any year
now we may witness a vast labour upheaval, having for its object the
seizure into the hands of the workers of all the instruments by which
wealth is produced, and their immediate employment by the workers for
the creation of wealth, no longer for individuals but for all. All existing
wealth to be at the same time confiscated, communalised, invested in

trustees, guardians of the welfare and well-being of the whole people, for all without exception.

So the miners paying no royalties, profits, or dividends, to any men, would dig out and send up all the coal needed by these nations, the railway men carry it wherever it was required, and the seamen having taken possession of all shipping would ply to and from foreign lands, bringing imports and carrying exports, and farmers released from rent would raise food and send it to the great centres of population, and all would work for all, and the production of wealth freed from the super-incumbent weight of capitalism would spring forward advancing as with leaps and bounds.

Prince Kropotkin[6] has, in his "Conquest of Bread", drawn an alluring picture of the happy condition of the people, all the people, including even the dispossessed classes, on the morrow of such a Syndicalistic Revolution.

Now, I do not say that such a revolution, and eventuating so, is beyond the power of man to achieve. All things are possible, and still, as ever, "God moves in a mysterious way His wonders to perform."[7] But you will observe that such a revolution, and eventuating so, would be the fulfilment of the all great prophesies, the realization of the visions of Isaiah and Virgil and our own Shelley, also of one greater than any.

[*The Irish Worker*, 23 November 1912]

To get money is hard; to create wealth is easy—easy and also delightful; for we are so made that we rejoice in creation. Then what is labour—as Nature made it—but creative activity? As Nature made it, not as man has perverted and degraded it. Even to-day do the toiling millions find any difficulty in creating wealth? Could not our builders, for example, build three times as many houses as they do to-day and three times as good, sound and enduring?

There is not a doubt of it. They would rise at once to the occasion. They would draw in those unemployed masons, bricklayers, carpenters, hodmen, &c., upon whom they now look sourly as blacklegs.[8] They would admit apprentices freely. They would rise to the demand with the same alacrity with which schoolboys start from their beds when the masters announce an unexpected holiday, with a glorious paper-chase in the country, finishing with a grand picnic on some heathery hillside, when the boys, looking from their dormitory windows, see the line of waggonettes and horses, and the hampers covered with white cloths secure in their places on the cars.[9]

Would not our builders, master-builders and men respond with some such alacrity to such a demand? Would they not reply?—"Yes, surely. We're ready. We'll build you houses, good, sound and enduring by the hundred, the thousand; you paying us our wages regular."

And they would do that, though to-day the wage-slaves are working under the curse of the Prophet. "The curse of the Prophet! What is that?"

"Ye shall build houses and others shall inhabit them."[10]

You know the children of the men who have built Dublin, its great houses and palaces, and the countless lovely villas with which Dublin is girdled, live in hired rooms and hired, cramped little cottages, tenancy to end, and the inhabitants to be cast into the street if a fortnight's rent is unpaid.

And you are all under that curse in all your work, whether it be transport or manufacture, agriculture, mining, or what-not. You create, make, fashion, carry to and fro for others, and for others who don't thank you.

"Why should we?" they say. "Don't we pay them?"

And the curse which lies heavy on you to-day will lie heavier upon you to-morrow and upon that vast and growing mass of the weak, sick, broken; upon those who have fallen out of your marching ranks and into those gulfs lying on either side of the road which your army of employed and employable still hold.

And I say to you as earnestly as I ever said anything in my life, that you, you must take up the cause of the poor, the weak, the broken, the unemployed and unemployable (?). For you the way of escape, the way to liberty, freedom, final victory lies here, and here only. You must take up the cause of the fallen. You, still strong and unbroken, employed and wage-receiving men and women, you, who are knit together in your powerful fraternal unions, you must lift up these fallen ones. You, you must show them pity and do them justice. No one else will. None of the classes will—not even the richest of them. They have been tried. They will not and they cannot; and neither will the State which they run.[11]

You alone can. It is your duty to do it, and it is within your power to do it. Also it is your interest to do it. Freed so from the competition of those whom you call blacklegs would not your wages rise? They would and immediately. They would rise as naturally as the tide rises in Dublin Bay. Your conditions would improve as naturally as the race of the country improves in the months of Spring. No fighting, no fury, no intimidation, no bruisings and maimings of famished blacklegs, no suffering for your women and children as now, when you attempt that desperate remedy, the strike. And what can you get even by successful strikes? A beggarly shilling or half-a-crown a week, soon discounted by the rise of the price of necessaries;

discounted, too, in divers other ways. At the best a wretched, beggarly thing even for you, the employed, the strikers. Of what avail for the unemployed, for all the poor broken people, while the sorry pittance implied in a victory is only an incentive to the competitors for employment roaming forever around you like wolves around Russian travellers in winter time.

To create every kind of wealth is easy. I only took the building of solid houses meant to last as an example. Then, to meet a great and sudden demand, you might build rapidly and in numbers good houses to shelter two generations.

I saw myself last summer two skilled men and a strong boy, and within a single week erect and equip an excellent three-roomed bungalow. It overlooked a beautiful valley traversed by a stream, like silver, well stocked with trout. Land fit for cultivation was attached and a feathery "winterland" good for sheep with an acre or two of turf bank hard by.

I hope your young people have not forgotten the old ideal of love in a cottage. It is a great deal better, believe me, than love in a palace.

And this lovely cottage, fit home for any young couple in the land, was put up within a week by two men and a boy. How many such cottage-homes for our young people caught in love's nets of gold—how many such and only at that rate of speed, the slow speed of hirelings will be erected by your building brigade?—say 500 strong young men and lads, perfectly free, rejoicing in their work and their happy comradeship, joking, laughing, singing at their work, gladder than the dancing waves of the sunny sea?

In one year more than 8,000 beautiful, commodious homes for near seventeen thousand happy lovers, loyal to each other and surely loyal to the great and generous Commonwealth to which they owe that felicity, to which they owe everything. For loyalty is a passion as natural to us as the passion of the love of life, deeper than the love of life. Only give men the chance and you will find that it is so. Found your Commonwealth of the free in that faith and "the gates" of capital will not prevail against it.[12]

You cannot liberate yourselves while you leave the unemployed and the broken and destitute—including you and your children perhaps to-morrow—in their present fearful conditions. You cannot give employment and a full and honourable maintenance without land, lands and their equipment. You cannot get land and their equipment without money, and at the beginning a great deal of money. You cannot get money except from the people—from the people in the first instance. Then the people will not support you in an enterprise so new, unprecedented and of such magnitude and with a revolutionary look so vast unless you touch their hearts and fire their imaginations. This, in a nutshell, is what I have been trying to put before you. The difficulties are immense, but not all what you suppose them to be. There are no material difficulties; none worth talking or thinking about. The way is clear. The difficulties are in your own minds—minds obsessed, held, steeped and saturated with the thought if you individually had money it would raise you out of the pit and set you free. Your minds are at this moment incapable of the thought that by a combined effort you could and would raise all out of the pit and lay the foundations of that social republic and Commonwealth of the free of which to-day you only dream. It will not come of its own accord or as the consequence of a few Parliament-made laws or of a mad orgy of incendiarism and murder. It will come only to the understanding and the brave, who have prepared themselves to meet it.[13]

[*The Irish Worker*, 23 November 1912]

The external revolution must be preceded and accompanied by an internal revolution. With your present mind you cannot conduct a revolution which would issue in anything but destruction. How could you? Don't you love, worship, and trust in money with a passion as strong as that which drives the capitalist? You know you do. Therefore, as opportunities and temptations multiply around you, multiplying around you just because you are leaders, you will be drawn aside, seduced, corrupted by the men who possess in vast masses the thing which secretly you adore. Then it puts forth its allurements in countless, cunning ways. Is it not the god of the whole earth, and matchless in sorceries? However upright, straight and honourable you seem to yourselves to-day to be, and are, it will buy you or break you; buy you when you become worth buying.

Without that prior and accompanying internal revolution you will never conduct to any good end an external revolution. And yet this internal change of heart, and mind, and outlook is not really so difficult as it would appear. It involves no more, to begin with, on your part than a perfectly clear understanding and a sincere conviction that this thing— money—which now devastates civilisation and demands annually its millions upon millions of human victims is not a good thing at all but an evil, and only to be valued as an absolutely necessary instrument, by the wise use of which men may escape from its all-but-infinite power.

I fear I have occupied too much of your space. With the Editor's kind permission I shall write a few words next week and so end. [14]

Just one thing more upon which you might meditate, I think with advantage, in the meantime. What do you think was the first word in the proclamation of the "good news" of Christianity on the earth? It was a single Greek word, metanoeite,[15] which means only change your minds, your ways of looking at things. Yet this one word led on to those tremendous utterances which the nations of Christendom would so like to see erased from where they stand and blotted out from the memory of mankind.

[*The Irish Worker*, 12 October 1912 resumed]

Would it not? "All for all," "all for each and each for all"! Would not that be the Millennium, the return to Paradise, the establishment of Christ's Kingdom upon Earth? And are not we, as we stand to-day, and without preparation, fresh from our brawls and ructions, our intestine and international hatreds always on the very edge of murder—hatred, you know, is murder—our tramplings on the weak and our salaamings to the strong, our universal, individual, and personal love of money and trust in it—are we not, as we stand, without purification and expurgation, very likely denizens and citizens of that Land of Promise, that Heaven upon Earth.

There may—for, again, all things are possible, and God lives though men forget the fact, or think He is dead—there may arise out of the deeps of our nature, such a tide of lofty aspiration, of courage, human and humanitarian enthusiasm, love of justice, love of kind, as will, at the same time, purge all hearts and sweep all forward to new and unimagined heights where the vision shall be an actual and living reality. But in the meantime it remains a vision. And it is with this "meantime", this actual present and this now and with people such as we, to-day, are that you have to deal, not with visions; and this vision cannot be converted into a reality, by calling it Syndicalism, which is in fact, only the French for trade-unionism, *Syndicat* being nothing but the French for a trade-union.

If you think otherwise, if you think that the reign of "all for all" is attainable through a[16] violent revolution, imagine for a moment a revolutionary committee sending forth its command to the farmers of Ireland to forward at once to the great cities trains laden with good food, eggs, butter, poultry, corn and meat, freely, joyfully and abundantly, because the day of "all for all" "all for each" and "each [for] all" has arrived.

Imagine such a call for made, not as the outcome of a great propaganda filling all hearts with a passionate yearning for justice and kindness and unity, infusing everywhere a spirit of glorious self-sacrifice for the realization of a divine idea, but as the issue of a violent revolution, and you will see that Syndicalism, glorious as a dream, is not attemptable, in fact, now and to-day, not by responsible and sober-minded men. And I say it while believing in this dream of the ages, dream of so many poets and prophets, and in its ultimate realization. For I perceive, considering the mind and heart of man, that we were made for that very social state which the word Syndicalism suggests, and for no other; made for mutual service not for mutual plunder, mutual hurt, and that this is as certain as that we were made physically to walk upright not on four feet like the animals. For all Nature is steeped in Intention, in purpose.[17] As Nature made the Earth for man and man for the Earth, made the Air for us to breathe, and equipped us with lungs for breathing it, made the blessed Light for us to see and gave us eyes to see it with: so it is equally certain that she made that happy state for us and us for it. And it is a bad sign of the time the general tendency to cry down every thought and aspiration which aims in this direction, for there is no murder like the murder of Hope. This dream of the ages is being dreamed again in our time,[18] and all I would say to you is—"While you look to the Paradise gleaming on the horizon take heed, too, of the ground on which you are planting your feet." For there is a way surely leading towards the realization of the great dream, a way made by God and Nature, and which we might have seen long since and long since have travelled, but for a certain spell by which men's minds are bound and their perceptions confused.[19]

How else can it be except through the power of a spell, a fascination, a sorcery, that you, hundreds of millions of you, working, working, making, creating, producing, transporting, such hosts upon hosts of brave and understanding men, are in such miserable subjection to and dependence upon a few thousands in no way better than yourselves: worse? Look at

Pierpont Morgan's face;[20] you will find it in any recent Encyclopaedia. And the subjection is not a noble subjection such as you once paid to a brave Peerage, a magnanimous chieftainry, in the old, wild fighting times, but a vile, forced subjection to mere monsters of opulence whom you yourselves have generated, created, and whom from day to day you sustain. How can it be otherwise? You are simply spellbound, victims of a glamour, of some fatal fascination by which all your higher faculties are numbed and your wills paralysed. For there is actually in this mysterious world such a thing as glamour. The rabbit on the ground, the bird on the bough, though well able to scamper or to fly, cower helpless before the gleam of eyes of the approaching reptile. Look with steady gaze at this astonishing subjection of hundreds of millions of men to a[21] few who prey upon and devour them; said few deteriorating day by day, all but smothered under the accumulations of opulence which you keep piling upon them. I speak of other countries such as England and America, for, thank God, we are all still tolerably poor in our own much favoured land, and I address you Irish because I think you will best understand, and I want you to be the first to break the spell and give the world a lead.

Look with steady eyes on this thing, the millions working furiously like madmen or devils for the depravement of the few, their unnervement, inevitable degeneration as fast as they emerge. You must not imagine for a moment that the rich are happy and enjoy a great felicity. Dives and his paid friends and pampered dependents, male and female, have their own world of "torment" perhaps worse than yours, appearances notwithstanding. They, too, are held by the spell though it emanates from them and is maintained largely by their apparent felicity.

You know that you are the victims of an oppression descending on you from the greed for more, and ever more money, of those who hold the Earth, source of all wealth, who own all the machineries and mechanisms and labour-saving contrivances, own the tools of the workers, own the capital and the credit, own your food and drink, clothes and houses, all the material things necessary for life, and which things are translatable and are hourly translated into money: are, in fact, money. For those things without which life is impossible give to money its vast irresponsible and all but infinite power. Money, the love of it, the hunger and thirst for it, the belief in it, the faith in it, the worship of it as if it were a God!—this is the oppressor. You know it, often say it and write it, are furious about it, half mad with a most righteous indignation about it.

And now like brave men look into your own hearts, and what do you find there?

Is there not something there, coiled but fearfully alive, though you are silent about it?

The passion, whose devastating power you see and rue in the great world that surrounds you, is in your own hearts. The God has a private sanctuary there where he is welcome and most devoutly worshipped. The modern working man is held down by his own personal subjection to the love of money.

Is there any escape from this net which seems to hold us all in its entanglements? If there were not I would not be addressing you, I would imitate many well-meaning friends and acquaintances who say:—"The thing is incurable, the tangle inextricable. Don't incur useless trouble. Let us lead our own lives as innocently and humanely as we can. That Social Revolution and Hell upon Earth, however inevitable, may not come in our time."

[*The Irish Worker*, 19 October 1912]

We are all caught and entangled in this net of seeming necessity which the power of money has woven around us and which lets not one of us escape. Without it we cannot live a life worth living. Without it we cannot even exist. Therefore, we all love money, and with the same kind of passionate instinct by which we are compelled to love life. The love of money proceeds from the same root as the love of life. Therefore it is always a surprise to me to see how honest and upright, kind and generous men can be nevertheless.

Now, distinguish between two passions—the passion of the love of life and the passion of the love of money. The love of life is of Nature, comes from the very deepest depths of our being; the love of money is not of Nature; it is a necessity imposed upon us by man. Then what man made he can unmake, just as he made and again unmade those demon things to which he sacrificed himself and in whose honour burned even his own children.

But was there ever any idol or devil to whom we offered such holocausts of victims as we do this? No! Though history tells of one[22] to whom were sacrificed 80,000 human victims in a single week. But those sacrificers took care to present to the god victims well fed and fat and in good liking. We offer ours in vastly greater numbers lean, pallid, and gaunt. I say "we," for we are all worshippers, and the dreadful god has his altar in every heart. Don't rave against the rich, against capitalists, companies, trusts, financial magnates. You can't change them; they are as they are. Let us blame ourselves. We are our own masters, supreme over our own minds. There, or nowhere, lies our chance. Chance! It is more than a chance; it is a certainty. But before you take, or can take, that first step to which I invite you, you must see this being, money, the money-god, not as he is seen and explained to us by his high priests and scribes as no more than an innocent "medium of exchange", and a "necessary standard of value", but as a man-devouring monster. Also you must perceive that you yourselves by your personal love of money, however innocent and even laudable it may seem to you, by your individual appreciation of the comforts, satisfactions, and delights which its possession confers, are yourselves the sustainers and maintainers of his terrible power. And the beginning of your freedom—which will be also ours—is not the first overt step and act upon your part but just this perception, and the self-conquest following upon that perception.

I, as well as you, believe in the great Commonwealth;[23] but I know that we cannot take one march in that direction without first breaking the now all-but-almighty power of this grand enemy of man.

I don't say at all, remember, that its power ought to be or can be abolished; only that its extreme and all-but-infinite power over men's lives should be checked and arrested, which is very possible.

And I differ in this from all the men of light and leading who surround me. They would teach more intelligent and profitable ways of serving the god. I, if I can, will teach how his power can be broken and the passion of the love of him expelled from men's hearts. And the time has come for the preaching of such a doctrine, for men now begin to understand, as never before, the true nature of this "innocent medium of exchange," how it accumulates in such formidable masses. They see, too, with their eyes the vast havoc which it wreaks, the homes which it devastates, the ruin which follows, the roll and roar of its triumph wheels.

You think that through revolution the power of this thing will be broken; but indeed you are wrong. Being in men's hearts it will emerge again and re-establish its dominion.

You can, if you are determined to do so, drive such people into revolution, each with his own unpurged heart. But believe me when I say that at the other side of such a revolution, a revolution carried through by such agents, there are no happy Paradises, no lambs and wolves lying down together, no weaned child laying his hand on the hole of the asp.

Such an issue is impossible. Every millennium that I have ever read of was to be preceded by the binding of the devil. You don't think surely—do you?—that the devil is less alive when he assumes his very foulest shape, that of Mammon. You must break his power before you can take one true step forward in the march towards freedom, emancipation, towards that earthly Paradise which you desire to enter.

"But that", you will say, "is impossible". I believe it is very possible. If it be not possible, why do you dream of the great Commonwealth? But it is perfectly possible, here and now, and without any such a tremendous experiment as that which is involved in the shaking of the social order to pieces and the unchaining of all the wolfish passions which lie hidden in the depths of man's soul. For we have a devil in us, surely as surely as we have a guardian angel.

It is possible, and for that reason I am here and saying things which many will regard as foolish, and many as wicked; and I say these things, being, as I believe, as practical as most, knowing as well as you the immense desirability of money and all the beautiful spendings that inhere in notes and sovereigns.

You cannot, even by superhuman activity, leap off your own shadows, not while your bodies are solid or opaque. You cannot escape from subjection to the money-power while the love of money is in your own hearts. That it is, you know. Is there one of you who would not rise joyfully to the receipt of £1,000 or of £300 a year of the ground rents of Dublin, that is, from the exploitation of the earth, or as dividends in a great company arising from the exploitation of its ownership, of the ways and means of men's lives? So you would abandon your own order and join the ranks of those whom you now call tyrants.[24]

In ancient classic times the slaves enormously outnumbered the freeman, often by five to one, sometimes by ten to one, yet could never achieve their freedom. Why? Because slavery was in their hearts. The slave's personal ideal was not so much to be free as to be free and to have slaves of his own. So there was almost never a servile revolt, and never a successful servile revolt. One great slave uprising, which was led by the brave Spartacus, looked for a while like succeeding, but was put down. The conquerors in one day crucified 6,000 of the revolted slaves along the highway between Rome and Capua. Had Spartacus and the slaves conquered there would have been no social regeneration as a consequence; only a yet worse social state, the slave leaders emerging as new and worse slave-owners.

So in vain will you fling into a state of revolution the millions of the down-trodden and oppressed of our time. Not though you cry with all your hearts, "Down with the money-power! Down with the greedy bloodsucking capitalists!" while every one of the revolted, their orators, captains, advisers, and counsellors, have in their hearts the love of that very thing against whose tyranny they revolt—a love which has never been expurged or mitigated. Torrents of blood, *battues* of your enemies by you, of you by your enemies, great cities going up in flame, credit gone, millions slain by famine—fever will not bring you one step nearer, but incalculable distances away from that divine Commonwealth to which you aspire. That happy state now beginning to be the dream of the whole earth, will not arrive in whirlwinds of rage and fury. It will come quietly, perhaps by imperceptible approaches, like the dawn, and, like the dawn, heralded by glad songs.

Then, don't forget that the massed power of capital, with its thousand subsidiary interests and its multitudes of dependent persons, is capable of doing terrible things, and will do them whenever it is seriously alarmed. There is no savage beast so cruel as frightened capital. And your people, too, each with money in his heart, are quite willing to be bought. Capital, when it is thoroughly alarmed, will buy your champions and trusted ones, at high prices, no doubt, but will buy them, and of your rank and file hire, clothe, discipline, arm, and equip as many killers as it needs. Then, for a little blood shed by you, it will shed much, and for a little violence wreak a tenfold violence; as its way is: the cruellest thing under the sun.

The Parisian oeuvrier democracy killed a few people in hot insurrection; a very few. Vengeful capital slew, not in battle but in cold blood, some forty thousand of them, as I understand, men and women, and even little boys of twelve.

I don't say this to make you afraid. That would be impossible. When you have such a fierce and just wrath in your hearts no such reminder of the power of your enemy could frighten you. I say this in order that you may clearly understand the nature of the foe and the power of the latent forces which he can bring into action.

I would have you circumvent him with a wisdom as of the serpent, outflank him, strike at his line of communications, compel him to shift from his strongly entrenched positions, force him to occupy others more assailable. I don't want you to rush at him in headlong fury like a bull, like those brave misguided Arabs charging the British Army at Omdurman,[25] only to be mown down in their thousands like swatches of reaped wheat. For I perceive that the money power, in some ways surprisingly intelligent and astute, is, in others, astonishingly stupid. You have the clear subtle Celtic intellect.[26] I want you to bring that, too, into action. Some one, you know, before our time recommended the wisdom of the serpent combined with the innocence of a dove.[27] I would have you bring to this war as much fire and enthusiasm as are in you; but also amid all your fire to preserve an intellect as cold and clear as pure ice.[28] Always when tempted to the direct attack remember those white swathes in the field of Omdurman.[29]

Remember this, too. These people, who hold by a cling to the skirt of capital and land—I refer now to the middle classes—are really quite human like yourselves. If reduced to poverty they would be labour men and Socialists just like you. They are only men and women who, being filled with an infinite and life-long terror of poverty, are, or will be, maddened at the thought of losing their money.

This terror, the terror of poverty, holds them now in the camp of the great capitalist property-owners. They dread poverty a great deal more than your people do. They are farther removed from it; and so their excited and active imaginations draw for them more frightened visions of the sufferings and degradations which await them should they fall into the pit, the soundless gulf yawning to receive the fallen.

Such are nearly all the middle classes in spite of their nice suburban houses, their quiet and staid appearance (which is a mask), their National air of persons who occupy a safe and assured position in society. They are filled, most of them, with an ever-present, unspoken terror of that pit which is literally the hell of our times, and which is a great deal more real and more terrible to them than that other one remote and invisible about which they are willing to hear something a small part of one day in the week. They fear with an infinite fear that dread gulf of poverty, not indeed for themselves, very much, but for their children. Is this not unlike your own people?[30]

Is not your Celtic intellect sufficiently penetrating to understand that a good proportion of them now clinging fast to the skirts of strong capital, might be detached and come over to the labour cause actually or in sympathy. So you might teach them that they, too, are workers, working terribly hard for a poor and uncertain contemptuous pittance flung them by that proud massed capital of which they, like all workers, are the slaves of victims.

Let me here interpret something a little off the track of the argument, but which may, perhaps, help to indicate, if indirectly, that plan of campaign which I have in mind.

What follows I read in this paper. You will, doubtless understand the reasons for that boycotting of one of the best, brightest, and most welcome happenings of our time. It is a small instance of what yourselves may yet do on a far greater scale.

At Christmas, 1911, you, the Transport workers, at the cost of your Union funds, gave a good Christmas dinner, some roast beef and plum pudding, to a hundred or so of our poor sandwichmen.[31] Which of us has not witnessed, with a sinking of the heart, the mournful processions of that confraternity through our streets? To them a good Christmas dinner, roast beef and plum pudding! More. After dinner your girls brightly dressed, and with friendly and smiling faces came upon the scene in their youth and beauty, freshness, gaiety, and animation, and with songs and music enlivened the minds and cheered the heart of the poor sandwichmen, causing them, if only for one night, to forget their griefs, and to remember, if for one night, that there was in their hard world such a thing as kindness and in their gloomy world such a thing as grace and beauty.

These poor people are much too weak and poor to fight their own battle. But I can imagine you or some other powerful Union taking up their cause, the cause of the weak and fallen, and declaring to their employers that, if you are not able, at present, to put an end to this disgraceful weekly spectacle, which is such a reflection upon our common Irish manhood and such a shame to Ireland's capital, you are determined at least that those who profit by the degradation of those men shall pay them a living wage. There are ways and means by which you might make good such a threat, and that, too, with little expenditure of your funds.[32]

[*The Irish Worker*, 26 October 1912]

Here is a question upon your answer to which a great deal will depend; indeed everything will depend:

Have the unemployed a right founded in justice to employment, with a full and fair remuneration—and, in lieu of that, to a sufficient and honourable maintenance, not a dishonourable and degrading maintenance such as we now provide for them by our brutal and devilish Poor Law? You will say "Yes". So do I. So will all whose natural sense of justice is not perverted by the fear that the full concession of such a right will not by its consequent abolition of blacklegism and of the present ferocious competition of our working people with each other for employment, reduce the profits of capital, and plunge themselves into poverty. Nothing but this terror of those who now live upon the exploitation of labour, prevents or retards the concession of that right. They resist the concession, not through any radical inhumanity, callousness and cruelty on their part, but through fear—fear which is the basest of the passions. It is a passion which, more than any other, obscures the intellect, hardens the heart, and sears the conscience. In a certain sense their fear is not altogether unnatural; for, beyond a doubt, the concession of that right, in full, would lead, and rapidly, to a social revolution carrying all forward, and by an immense stride, towards that promised Kingdom of God on earth and away from this present dominion of the devil. This seeming all-but-Almighty power of the devil in his form of Mammon, is maintained to-day, not by any inherent strength and wisdom of his own, but just through the refusal of that right, the consequent murderous competition of the working people, for employment, and the resulting usurious profits of the exploiting capitalists.

Observe, in passing, a grandly hopeful and inspiring aspect of the situation. It is this: Fear, which is the meanest, the most cruel and the most terrible of the passions, is just that one human passion which is most easily mitigated and most easily abolished and quenched. The little child in an agony of terror at the dark is at once pacified, and sinks back into sleep hearing only just one quiet and reassuring word from his mother. The people who now live upon their usuries, that is, upon your exploitation, and see no other way of living, are just like children in dread of the dark. To them the situation is all dark and terrible. Allay that terror, and you may yet find that not only the middle classes, but even the Diveses of the earth are not so bad after all; are, in fact, quite human—like yourselves. At all events, don't frighten them any more than they are frightened at present. Then you are in fact frightening them, I believe, quite unnecessarily, to-day, by threatening to deprive them of their property by direct violence or by violent legislation. And [I] tell you that it is a very dangerous game and, indeed, in every way wrong, such a taking away from men, no matter what the justification, of that which they have been accustomed to regard as their property.[33] We have never been told that the violent shall inherit the earth; but assured upon very good authority that the gentle shall inherit the earth.

If you think and consider and give your understandings fair play, you will find that the Sermon on the Mount is not a bundle of absurd paradoxes at all, but a most plain and scientific and divine statement of certain truths. "The employment of the unemployed!" The peaceful and gradual solution of the whole of this tragical, social problem seems to be contained in it. There is now before Parliament a poor little Bill bearing this title. It is very poorly urged by your Labour Party, and is ignored, where not jeered at, by the Press. Nevertheless, the demand which is contained in it is one pregnant with immense issues, and has had a great history, to which [I] now invite your earnest attention.

In the Forties of the eighteenth century, our Bishop Berkeley, distressed in his humane mind at the frequent sight of tramps and beggars upon all our highroads, called upon the Irish aristocracy to employ these unemployed, to feed, clothe and shelter them "well", and to set them upon the creation of wealth, both for their own sustentation and for the general good of the whole community. The Irish gentry, at the time in full command, were willing enough to do many other things which their great Bishop invited them to do, and also profited themselves greatly, too, by following his advice. But, concerning this one practical suggestion of his, they were silent. They said nothing and did nothing.

You can guess, Why.

The great Bishop might as well have walked down from his palace at Cloyne to the seashore and addressed the dead waves of the Atlantic at Ballycotton.

In the thirties of the nineteenth century, when the Whigs were fastening their devilish Poor Law upon the neck of these nations, the poet, Wordsworth, at the time popular, famous and respected, entered a powerful argumentative protest against that system.[34] He maintained that the British man, the Irish likewise, had an indefeasible right, in Nature and in law, to a full and sufficient and honourable maintenance in lieu of employment and wages. The governing classes—busily engaged as they were in the exploitation of land and capital and labour—quite ignored that powerful protest. They made him Poet Laureate, praised the "Beech Gatherer", "We are Seven" and "The Daffodils";[35] but took care at the same time to fasten down their Poor Law System tight upon these countries with its denial of that right founded upon nature, and in law, reading back to magna charta [*sic*] and beyond, to the days of Edward the Confessor, as Wordsworth powerfully maintained.

The poet might as well have delivered his argument to the babbling Rotha which ran by his Cumberland Cottage, or declaimed it to Grasmere's reeds and sedges.[36] There was no public discussion at all upon that powerful protest. It was simply ignored, so that time nearly swallowed it up in oblivion. I lighted upon it myself by accident.

When Tom Paine published his "Rights of Man" they did not at least boycott it or enjoin silence in their Press. No. They advertised it hugely and filled the world with their execrations. Why?

They felt that Wordsworth's "Rights of Man" was a serious danger to their position, but that that other "Rights of Man", with its accompanying Deism and denial of the proverbial inspiration of the Scriptures, was a help. It enabled them to stand out before the foolish many as the champions of orthodoxy.[37]

A few years later Wordsworth's great theme was taken up by a greater man—Thomas Carlyle. In words of blazing indignation he called, loudly enough almost to wake the dead, upon England's possessing and governing classes to do this thing, to employ the unemployed, to do it at once and without a moment's delay, to do it intelligently, thoroughly, bravely and heroically.[38] He told them that it was their duty to do it, as it was the clear right of the poor to have it done. Also, he declared to them that, if they did not do it, they and England with them would go down amid such whirlwinds of horrors and terrors as universal history had not yet exhibited upon any of her lurid pages. Almost literally this great-minded, unpaid champion of the poor, and at the same time of all England's nobler traditions, thundered and lightened at the possessing and ruling classes about this thing. All his many books had the same end in view. They are all, direct or indirect, appeals to the reason and conscience of England to take up this work, this first, as the first step towards the salvation and regeneration of England. This was the one thing—the one and only thing— that Carlyle asked England to do.

England, in reply—if indeed England ever made any articulate reply—only remarked that Carlyle was a very eloquent person, possessed a fine gift of satire, &c., &c., but unfortunately was unpractical.

He was succeeded by the noble John Ruskin, who in the fifties, sixties, and seventies, of the last century continued in many ways to reassert Carlyle's doctrine. And I am glad to note in all labour papers a continual recognition of the generous and unbought labours of these brave preachers, as well as frequent quotations from their works. Both of them thought that the rich were too stupid to understand. It was not quite so. The rich—at least the brains-carriers of the rich—perceived that if there were no unemployed, no destitute persons looking for employment, wages would necessarily go up and profits go down, that they themselves would in consequence cease to exist, and that the first step would be taken towards a radical reconstruction of society.

They were right. But what they failed to perceive and what their successors there and here fail to perceive is that in a world like this, made by infinite goodness and wisdom, Right is always the grand stand-by for men and for nations, and for the rich as well as the poor, and that Wrong, sooner or later, ends in misery and destruction.

I don't wish any unhappiness to befall the classes. I know them too well and understand their many troubles too intimately to desire in any way to add to their afflictions. But I see clearly that the same road which leads to your emancipation leads also to theirs. I believe that they would see it themselves if they could only give their understandings fair play. This they cannot do at present. Their minds are too darkened, confused and obscured by that basest of all the passions—habitual and lifelong fear of poverty. Carlyle laughed at the Englishman's hell—poverty. It is the Irishman's, too. Unexpressed, unseen, unheard, this consuming fear is devastating the lives of the classes. And I say again that the very best thing you can do for your own people is just to mitigate, perhaps abolish, that fear.

I advise you, the leaders of Irish Labour, to press along this line of advance with all your power. It is the line of least resistance and of greatest results. Doing so you concentrate the greatest amount of force possible upon a point which is necessarily the very weakest in defence. For who will openly maintain that the unemployed have no other right than the right to walk into the workhouse?

But here arises a difficulty which fortunately only seems to be insuperable. The rich won't employ the unemployed; they are afraid of cutting through the branch upon which they themselves sit. Neither will the State; it is the organ and agent of the rich. If, by agitation, you drive the State into doing it, the State will only seem to do it. The State, the agent and organ of the exploiting classes, will never do it cordially, thoroughly and sincerely. I once visited one of the State's "Labour Colonies", and shall never visit another. I saw the men there degraded and conscious of their degradation.

What remains? I say it boldly and with confidence. Do it yourselves. I see that you have the financial and other material ways and means of doing it, and that nothing is really wanting upon your side except just the heart to dare and do. You can change the face of the world if you do this.

You must remember that while individually unpropertied and having little cash to spare, you are, collectively and *en masse*, the potential wielders of enormous financial power. Here, as elsewhere, the pennies and sixpences of the millions mean a colossal capital, a mighty revenue; if only you, the leaders, can kindle their enthusiasm and fire their imaginations by setting before them the prospect of a certain and mighty advance, not partial and limited, but limitless and "all along the line".

I hope to show you, nay, to demonstrate, how a few thousands of your young people equipped with land, its boundless fertilities, equipped with the astonishing results of modern science, and with our miraculous modern machineries and labour-saving contrivances, how such a few thousand of our young people working, not as wage slaves, but as free men and women, might produce with ease and with pleasure, too, all the necessaries of life and every rational kind of wealth needed by many millions! Indeed, I perceive that if you don't annex and master these machineries, they are going to master you, and that they mean either your complete emancipation or your complete enslavement; the return of chattel slavery on the earth. One or the other.

[*The Irish Worker*, 2 November 1912]

The abolition of unemployment, abundant and varied opportunities of occupation, the provision, in an ample and honourable manner of the necessaries of life for all would have these effects. It would break the power of capital, to exploit and oppress, to grind and impoverish, leaving it free otherwise to do everything great, salutary and beneficent which may be in its power to do. It would abolish in the mind of the classes and in the mind of the masses that extreme dread— nay terror—of poverty now everywhere oppressing men's souls like a veritable nightmare. It would proportionately reduce the really insane passion of the love of money which makes men so savage and remorseless in their dealings with each other, and against which all the great prophets and preachers have preached, so far in vain. For it is as true to-day as it was when the great Apostle said so, that this love "is the root of all evil".[39] But while money means life and the want of it means death, it is useless to say such things. Let men have the assurance that they will never—they and their little ones and their parents and kindred and dependents— never be plunged into the bottomless gulfs of destitution, and this inhuman, anti-social passion will quietly pass out of their hearts. Then, and not till then, will man be free to show and prove what, he actually is, what God and Nature made him. They have made him upright and brave and kind; also have made him a being who naturally delights in every kind of creative activity. Is he not made in the Creator's image?

Is it so very difficult to supply employment for the unem-ployed and the necessaries of life for all? It does not really seem to be such a tremendous great feat after all, assuming that you had in your possession the various means and instruments of production.

If you had the necessary agricultural land for the production of food—land well equipped with stock, plant, tools and agricultural machineries, creameries, orchards, fruit gardens, &c., &c., you will understand generally how the free, glad labour of volunteers, associated in groups, working with zeal, alacrity and pleasure, would produce, and in vast masses, all the necessary food needed by multitudes of people otherwise employed. You must agree with this, for it is your position as socialists when you demand the ownership and control of the means of production. Then, as believers in freedom, liberty, you are illogical, inconsequent in your reasoning, if you can, at the same time, believe too in forced labour; in men being driven to work like the ancient chattel slaves, or the wage slaves of civilization. I hope you see this clearly. If you do, hold fast by that perception, and never, for a moment, let it pass from your minds. Nature meant man to be free, neither a driven slave nor a slave driver.

Never let a capitalist Press or the conscious or unconscious, paid or unpaid friends of capitalism bully you out of it with sneers and jibes: that is out of the perception that in Freedom man is seen at his greatest and best, even as a mere wealth-producer. You know yourselves how his powers are crippled, even in wage-slavery, which is in itself an immense advance upon chattel slavery. Seeing this hold fast by the perception. There is a truth here which is central, cardinal, vital, and essential. If you forget it you will be lost, for you will then be compelled, inevitably, to adopt its opposite, the principle of your exploiters, that man is by Nature so idle and bad that he cannot be got to work at all except by force. All tyranny and all slavery are latent in this vile and false doctrine. You may know its falsehood because it is a favourite theme of capitalism grown articulate through its Press and of all people who are capitalistically inclined. Capitalism keeps the road mainly through the diffusion and maintenance of mean notions about human nature. You at least ought not to be its aids and allies in that vile game.

You will, urban men, more easily understand how, if upon such land, you had the necessary machineries and labour-saving contrivances, you could produce with little labour, and that volunteered, abundantly and in vast masses more than enough for all. That, too, is your position as socialists, when you say "Give us the instruments of production". Now, your people, however poor individually, are, collectively and *en masse*, possessors of a vast financial power, a power as great as that of any of these capitalistic companies which are now grinding you to destruction, living and feeding literally on your flesh and blood, and more and ever more desperately and greedily as year follows year. And they can't help it. Please remember this, that they can't help it; and also that they are composed— these exploiting capitalists and capitalistic companies—of men and women, children, too, exactly like yourselves, with hearts and minds and sorrows and hopes like yours. If you prick them they will bleed.[40] They, too, are driven by the same god or fiend, who has us all in thrall. Hate him or it as much as you like, as much as you can. Don't hate the men, women and children who to-day chance to be the wielders of the power of capital.

Buy the land and buy the machineries, and through the free, glad, enthusiastic creative activities of men and women, lads and maidens, of happy girls and merry boys, pour forth wealth in such masses, such torrents, that no one will care even to keep an account of its distribution or whether it is consumed by the good or the bad, the worthy or the unworthy; any more than we keep an account to-day of the good water drunk by thirsty men and horses at our drinking fountains. Make milk as free for our children as water is to-day. Make all the necessaries of life—the necessaries first—as free for all as are to-day the blessed light and the sweet air. For you can do it if you like; do it with ease and with pleasure, delight and satisfaction. Think and consider. You can do that—can you not?—far more easily than you to-day work for the exploiter, than you to-day labour and grind and slave and suffer and perish raising wealth, for the few,

at the same time for their depravement and your own progressive enslavement.

Now, this the glad creation of wealth by all for all has
been indeed always possible, and has been actually and in a
considerable degree realized half consciously among some
happy nations in their primitive simplicity, peoples who just
obeyed the natural instincts which are in us all. I refer, amongst
others, to those little pre-historic communes and socialistic
clan republics which Europe was once besprinkled all over as
the sky with stars. A beautiful example of such natural primitive instinctive socialism is supplied by the little independent
communal or semi-communal States of ancient Greece—
friendly, independent States with territories often as small as
the areas of our own parishes! It was in the early Hellenic
times when the Greek was young and in the dawn of his great
day, pious and simple and friendly and fraternal. It is a
beautiful story this of the young Greeks before they began to
degenerate[41] still dimly perceptible through the mists of
time[42]—a noble and even prophetic bit of human history. I
say prophetic because we must regard as such all examples
shown anywhere of "brethren dwelling together in unity".[43]

Such a free and glad production of wealth by all for all,
and each for each, and each for all, was, as I say, indeed
always possible; could man but have seen through the veil of
lies, deceits and idolatries which he has in some mysterious
manner woven around his own soul.

Always possible. But now! now! do you at all or fully realise
the range and extent of the stupendous powers which man's
brain and inventive capacity are bringing to his assistance in
the creation of wealth out of the rude materials supplied
by Nature.

There is a machine which puts forth a gigantic hand—a
hand which at one grasp takes up two tons of clay and gravel,
lifts that mighty load, carries it, and deposits it carefully in
a railway truck waiting for its reception; all within three
minutes, to the guidance of a single operator working handles.
The men who are so miraculously assisted in their labours by

this iron Titan receive no material benefit from its huge services no more than you, dockers, derive from the great cranes, or you, railway men, from the steam engine.

[*The Irish Worker*, 9 November 1912]

I have just been reading a description of a spinning machine which spins 340 miles of woollen yarn in one day, going day and night. In the accompanying photograph there is one girl, the tender and minder. That girl's great-grandmother with her spinning-wheel, which, too, was, in its way, a great labour-saving discovery, could not spin more than half a mile if so much in a long day. Yet this girl who, so assisted, spins at the rate of 340 miles a day is no better off, nay, in many ways, much worse off than her great-grandmother.

There are weaving machines which in a day will weave cloth enough to supply good tweed suits for a hundred men with a very little assistance from the human hand.

The bootmaking industry is not, I think, so far advanced. Yet, from inquiries which I have made in Leicester, I gather that one hundred boys and girls can turn out 300,000 pairs of boots in a year. Nor should I be surprised if the true number were nearer half a million. Where the old-fashioned shoemaker cut out the soles one by one laboriously with a knife, now a sole-cutter descends through a great pile of skins and in less than three minutes cuts out a hundred soles.

Pins are made by automatons; matches by machines which are all but automatons. A few girls equipped with the new machinery can turn out matches by the million.

Why multiply instances? You know as well as I do that the machine is superseding the man, and that the capitalist, mad about gain, is, as fast as he can, getting rid of men and substituting women and boys and girls. To-day he is doing his best to get rid of women, boys and girls and substitute automatons.

Then what are machineries without land upon which to plant them, on which to build your workshops, factories and living houses and from which to derive food. For employing unemployed land seems more necessary then anything else.

Science impelled by capital's driving power is directing its attention to the almost infinite food-producing capacity of the earth.

We know now that even child-labour if well directed, can do marvellous things upon the earth. What follows here is an extract from one of the State papers of the United States.

"By putting in a new crop as soon as one was harvested school-garden boys under twelve years raised on the 16th of an acre 336 bunches of radishes, 110 bunches of onions, 368 heads of lettuce, 89 bunches of beet, 8 bushels of beans, 7 bushels of tomatoes, 7 bunches of carrots, 1 peck of turnips, besides nasturtiums and petunias, many boxes of which were sent to the hospitals of the city.—U.S. Bulletin No. 160."

Now, multiply these figures by 16—it is worth the trouble—to find the produce of an acre so tilled: 5,376 "bunches of radishes", and so on. Again, multiply the resulting figures by 100 to find the produce of 100 acres of our good Irish earth tilled so—that is, by child-labour under instruction. You will then see that a small proportion of our Dublin school children, working a very small proportion of this, your fertile County of Dublin, would produce all the necessary plain vegetables required by vast numbers of people.

Observe, too, that work of this kind, always in moderation, is a necessary part of the education of children. What can be better for little boys and girls, their bodies and minds, than productive, well-directed physical activity in the open air? Child-labour driven for gain by the capitalist is perhaps the most tragical thing under the sun. Child-labour may be one of the most beautiful sights on the earth as well as an essential and necessary part of the child's physical, mental and moral education.

Is there any reason why our children might not grow and gather and transfer to centres of distribution, and by hundreds of tons, fresh, juicy, wholesome strawberries and all manner of fruits, still as a necessary and also glad and delightful part of their education? Is there any reason why they should not grow, gather, grade and store good apples in the autumn for the year's consumption of our people? There is none?

Yet to-day in our great cities there are millions of children and grown persons, too, who almost never see on their tables a dish of fresh strawberries through all the sunny strawberry months, while huge vans laden with that delicious fruit, but owned by exploiters, roll daily past their doors. Why is this? How comes it that while the earth is of such limitless fecundity, and while the human hand and brain can perform such wonders, there is such ghastly want in our midst? Because the earth and everything else is exploited, all the natural avenues to the creation of wealth barred, in order that the great god—Mammon—may accomplish his purposes.

Indeed I sometimes think that our children alone—counting as children all boys and girls under 14 years—might produce, and that with joy, most of the necessaries of life for us all. I beg you to think of this when you make your own calculations. Consider the new agriculture in some of its other modern aspects.

There are machines driven by the newly discovered natural forces which will plough 10, 20, 30 acres in a day, one foot deep, two feet deep, three feet deep, according to the nature of the soil and the will of the operators. There are machines which will drive deep drains, flinging on either side clay, gravel stones, and even "boulders", as there are finely tempered chisels which cut through steel as if it were cheese. I have seen these chisels myself at work in Sheffield where, too, I witnessed the conversion, in half-an-hour, of some fifty tons of molten iron into ingots of pure steel, which was the work of perhaps a thousand men working for months in the pre-Bessemer days.

An intelligent, instructed boy or a girl, or an old man might govern many of those machineries sitting at ease, and working handles. In afforestation, holes for the planting of young trees are made by the explosion of dynamite cartridges, instantaneously and better than they can be dug by a strong labourer with a spade. I have seen a photograph of American farmers ploughing a great field by the explosion of dynamite cartridges. The cartridges are set in lines by a drilling machine and fired simultaneously. The explosion, I understand, not only turns up the undersoil thoroughly, but triturates it and spreads the fine particles evenly over the surface. Science is beginning to displace muscular humanity in the field as in the factory and workshop. And you can have these machineries either as your deadliest enemies or your most serviceable friends, allies and co-partners in the work of food production. They are potentially one or the other, deadly enemies or willing and most potent friends. Friends if you own them; enemies if you leave them in the hands of the exploiter.

It is well known that a cow, which in Ireland to-day requires for her sustenance some two acres of pasture beside winter food supplied by tillage upon a third, may be maintained upon one acre of well-tilled ground. But now I hear on good authority that one cow can be and is well kept on the produce of the third of an acre well cultivated. If that be so, you can produce six times as much milk from a given area by intelligent cultivation as is produced by our own graziers, who are satisfied with the spontaneous gifts of Nature, in other words, mere pasture or grass. Our Irish cows, too, waste nearly as much grass as they eat. Their great weight pressing upon four small hoofs destroys grass.

One hundred acres, therefore, so tilled might maintain a herd of 300 cows producing some three million pints of milk per annum. Make your own calculations; I only deal with things very generally, my object being only to indicate what indeed ought to be universally known, the astonishing fecundity of the earth. If you set out to make good milk free to all, is there any real difficulty in the way? There are always millions of little children about to become men and women, and who ought to have as much milk as they can drink and as much bread and oatmeal porridge and fruit, jams and puddings as they can eat.

As to cereals—we seem to be only at the beginning of a revolution. Some thirty bushels of wheat to the acre used to be considered a very good yield, forty bushels a record yield. This year an agricultural firm writes to say that they have upon one statute acre grown seventy-two bushels of wheat of the kind known as the "Essex Conqueror" (Review of Reviews, October 1912). It is one of those hardy, prolific, and disease-resisting varieties of oats and wheat bred by the Agricultural Department of the University of Cambridge on their experimental station in Cambridgeshire.

When you get to work ask that University to send you one of their trained students to preside over the cereal department of your estate and to start your own experimental station. He will be with you by the next boat, never niggling about terms. There are enthusiasts in every department of human activity; men who want nothing but a sufficient maintenance, the ways and means of action, and an honourable position.

You, the workingmen leaders of the Irish people, need know little yourselves; need only know that it is your function to break up and smash down the power of capital, to oppress.[44] This indeed you must know well, but need to know little else. You will have no difficulty in getting men and women fit to instruct, taking a wise lead in every department of activity and who will ask for no other remuneration than the wages and means of action, an honourable maintenance and an honourable position. Now, none of these things will cost you anything. Note in passing that in some direction or other we are all enthusiasts, all a little mad, and are all more eager for sympathy, consideration and honour than about our backs or our stomachs.

How many acres now will even a hundred lads—volunteers—well equipped with the necessary ways and means and machineries be able to cultivate without in any way distressing themselves? Ten thousand at the very least. Our young Canadians do far greater things than this. A hundred such lads might grow near a million of bushels of "the Essex Conqueror".

I have just seen a letter from an Irish farmer, who writes as follows:—

"With my potato-digger I can dig two Irish acres of potatoes in one day which would be the work of sixteen men armed only with spades."

The astonishing feats done by modern science and art in the world of manufactures and transportation are about to be repeated in agriculture. But if you don't own the land and don't own the wages and means and machineries, this great extension of the domain of human power will avail you as little as the steam engine has availed you, or the spinning jenny, or the power loom.

Some of you are thinking of free meals for children. Why not free and good household accommodation, which is almost as imperative as food? Why not decent clothing and good boots? But the cost of these things to-day, when everything is exploited, is prohibitive. The resulting taxation would swamp the greatest cities.

Turn where you will, you can make no real great advance in any direction in a world where everyone is in pursuit of money, and where in consequence everything is exploited. Yet you see from the instance of those little Washingtonian boys that even children can raise food in masses.

Because men experience such immense difficulty in making money they think that the creation of wealth must be difficult, too. It is not, but easy in the extreme. A young lady has just told me that she got this year from her hives 450 lbs. of honey, yet who, by keeping bees, can make enough money on which to live? And it is the same everywhere; easy to create wealth, very hard and growing harder every day to make money. It is a necessary and inevitable result of the universal and inevitable result of the inevitable rush for money, resulting in the exploitation of all things, beginning with land. When multitudes of people, most of them panic-stricken, rush for escape at one narrow entrance, a jam there is the sure result.

Get the land, get the machineries, aim not at money, but at the co-operative creation and generous diffusion of wealth, and you can produce wealth and pour it forth, oceans of it, without difficulty, nay, with joy and delight.

But while money rules, and every one is obsessed with the passion of getting it, and with the fear of not having it, this is impossible. Some people bolder and more understanding than the rest must break through the net. I have dreamed that it might be you, and if there are only a handful of you at first— only as many as might sit round a small table—hold the thought that to the brave all things are possible.

There is a grand line which runs through our Ossianic literature like a refrain:—

"We were nine men;
   We took captive the king and the Britains."[45]

I believe that nine men of the right kind could smash the money power and liberate mankind. For from the moment that they form that resolution, all kinds of visible and invisible allies and helps and assistances will come around them.[46]

If but a handful of you could move out, at the same time intelligently and fearlessly, to battle with this dreadful power, there can be but one result of such a war. For this dreadful power which appears to be all but Almighty, has in fact no more substance and reality than is possessed by a nightmare.

[*The Irish Worker*, 16 November 1912]

The fecundity—the astonishing productivity of the earth!

You are, urban men and women, in daily, hourly contact with the things that are dead, and have lost touch with the beautiful living forces of Nature, her generosities and charities, her astounding beneficence and munificence, her loving care for all her children and chiefly for her last, who are ourselves, wretched rebels as we are, who, at the first opportunity, fly from her sacred presence, pack ourselves together in cities and other congested [places and] prey upon each other like wolves driven mad with famine.

Knowing nothing of the earth, you have forgotten the earth's astonishing fecundity, though it so nearly and vitally concerns you. You will learn it again but only after you have bought it and begun to use it. For before you can employ the unemployed you must buy the earth as well as the machineries and labour-saving contrivances.

Have you realised at all what torrents of wealth the earth is ready and willing and eager to pour forth for you in return for a very little labour? Labour which is, in fact, no more than the burning of a pinch of incense in honour of her divinity; labour, too, which our common nature has made, for a great many of us, very pleasant, interesting and delightful. Consider what follows.

There are in this county two hundred and nineteen thousands of acres of the most fertile land in the world. Get ten thousand acres of it—even one thousand acres—and use that little scrap and scantling of our total twenty-one millions of acres for the glory of God and the service of man, the sustainment of the poor and afflicted and the advancement of Christ's kingdom on earth for the "coming" of which you pray—don't you?—thinking very little, I fear, about the meaning of the words which flow so sweetly from your lips.

And this grand domain of Ireland's capital is now waste.

Go up to Blessington by the steam tram, out by train toward Naas, out towards Navan, out Northward to Drogheda. Look round on all sides—what do you see? Grass, grass, grass—oceans of grass—the owners say it will not pay them to till it. Money here again bars the way. They are exploiting the beautiful earth and find the most profitable exploitation to be—just to let it remain as it is.

When it is yours, as I trust in God it yet will be, you will not exploit it. Will you not be fleeing from exploitation? You will turn your people on to it armed with the many and powerful weapons, the cunning ways and means with which modern science has equipped man and will cause it to yield what Nature meant it to yield.

You have not got it yet, nor the funds necessary for its purchase and equipment; but you have in the people of Ireland, and especially in the nobly idealistic Dublin democracy, an inexhaustible mine of living gold, better than those of Alaska and South Africa, ready to pour forth for you all that you need when you touch their hearts and fire their imaginations. You don't know yet what a wonder-working power is the imagination. But you must not forget that you have in Dublin perhaps the highest-minded, truest-hearted, most generous democracy of any of the great cities of the earth. Remember how they have stood always by the highest thought and idea presented to them; how they held by Parnell in his waning days.

A word about what this fecund Irish earth—what it may be got to yield when redeemed from its present grassy condition. A hundred acres will produce five hundred thousand pounds of strawberries, or seven hundred thousand pounds of gooseberries, three hundred thousand pounds of currants, 800 cwt. of nuts. And all this largely as a resultant of mere child labour under the direction of understanding and sympathetic elders. A few such women preferably would convert those cultivated acres into veritable Gardens of Eden for the children, with processions to and fro, bands, banners, and other arranged rural solemnities.

Children delight in activities, and especially when such are ordered and beautiful and of evident service and help to the grown-ups. A well-conditioned healthy child is never so happy as when useful. Then the bringing home and the grading, and the storing and the jam-making might easily be converted into a great pleasure to them as well as a great service to the community, while the moral and physical education therein implied would be incalculable.

Shake off this foul obsession of money now sitting in your souls like a nightmare, and such possibilities, and in a hundred directions, begin to reveal themselves.

The foregoing figures I have taken from a recently published Encyclopaedia. They only represent the results of old-fashioned fruit-gardening. But we are, in fact, only at the beginning of a revolution which will 'ere long double and treble present estimates by the productivity of land. The wonder-working brain of man is turning its flashlight eyes upon the earth, his mind realising its immense potential resources. At the same time the capitalist, too, is looking at the earth through those eyes and preparing to come into action with a view to exploitation. When he does, do you think food will be cheap and abundant? Not at all. He will send it forth to the ends of the earth wherever the markets are good. He will not be here to feed the Irish people. No nonsense of that kind will find a place in his practical head and business-like brain. Of heart, of course, he will have none. He will be here to exploit the earth and to make money.

Land is not dear in Ireland to-day. Indeed, I think that upon the whole it is cheap, considering that you can draw from it some six or ten times what the poor present proprietors can cause it to yield. Once the capitalist turns his attention to it, it will be very dear indeed. Therefore I would say the sooner you buy it the better; if indeed you do at all seriously think of employing the unemployed, of providing the necessaries of life for all, of taking practical steps towards the establishment of that[47] great Republic and divine Commonwealth of which you dream.

[*The Irish Worker*, 30 November 1912]

Whence this immense power of money? It is not necessary to look far. We cannot live, cannot even from day to day exist, without some portion of the produced wealth of the world. All wealth is produced directly or indirectly from the Earth. To-day the Earth is exploited, that is, held up by its owners against mankind for the highest possible price in money that they can be compelled to pay for its use. These, in their turn, necessarily demand the highest possible money-price from others for the wealth ready for consumption, like food, or the raw materials of such, like iron, timber, &c., &c.

Therefore, all wealth is exploited with an exploitation which starts from the exploitation of the Earth; and so everything that we need, even the prime necessaries of life, we can only get by money—the utmost amount of it that we can be compelled to give. So, money emerges having the power of life and death in its hands, and, being translatable quickly into both land and wealth, comes out too as an independent power able to exploit itself, and charge great interests (usuries) for its use.[48] The gigantic power of money which has made us all both mad and bad, springs from and is sustained by that immeasurable wrong which we, of Civilization, have committed upon ourselves by the gradual conversion of the divine Earth into a merchantable article. So, money little or much comes into our hands clothed with the power of that immeasurable wrong. Its power which makes the possession of it so delightful is a power rooted in wrong.

If I were addressing the classes I would enlarge upon the evil nature of the exploitation of the Earth. Speaking to you it is not necessary. You know well how evil it is, while a very little reflection will convince you that, though experience, the testimony of your senses, seems to prove that money is a good thing, reason declares it to be not good but evil.

You know that our senses often deceive us. I once saw what my eyes declared to be two gigantic animals, like tigers, charging at me. They were only setters answering my call, their size trebled by the mist. You thrust an oar into sunlit water and see the oar bent, though you know that it is straight. You see the sun rise, but you know that that is an ocular delusion caused by the spin of the Earth from west to east.

Our senses declare money to be a good thing; reason and knowledge contradict their testimony and pronounce it to be evil. It is in fact a necessary evil. Now the right use to make of a thing which is at the same time necessary and evil, and also possessed of enormous power, is to employ that power with a view to escape from its control. Armed with that power, the power of money, should the people support you, you can buy lands and their equipment, including, workshops and factories, machineries and labour-saving contrivances, and in those lands establish the Commonwealth of the free, of men, women, and children, escaped from the slavery in which you are to-day immersed, and looking back with mingled horror and joy upon the fearful conditions which surrounded them in the past.

In short you must buy freedom; and buy it through the medium of that very thing which is to-day crushing the life out of you. Let me give two illustrations of my meaning, when I say that money should be used with a view to escape from its power. A prisoner escaping from his dungeon traverses a tunnel charged with mephitic gases. It is the story of Red Hugh escaping from Dublin Castle.[49] Though he knows that the air is poisonous, does he cease to breathe? No. He fills his lungs as he goes with the mephitic atmosphere, and presses forward all he can, towards the outer air and liberty. He knows he is breathing poison, but the poisonous air which he breathes gives him power to escape. Were he to stay in that tunnel he would resemble a modern democracy, contented by consuming its wages, and not using those very wages with a view to escape from wage slavery.

A sailor finds himself alone in a boat on the wide seas; comrades dead; water gone. But there is a cask of sherry still in the boat. It is a story which I once read. Now the poor sailor must drink if he would live; therefore he drinks sherry. He knows that it is injuring him; he drinks it nevertheless sparingly; keeps his sails set, and plies the oar while ever his eyes scan the horizon. The sherry is killing him; he drinks it nevertheless, because he loves life and is eager for salvation.

If you understand clearly and know well the evil nature of money, you will not devote yourselves to acquiring it with a view to personal enjoyment. You will indeed long to possess it even in millions, but only in order that you may wield its mighty power to save yourselves and others, indeed save us all; for we are all everyone of us caught in this Devil's net.[50]

And don't be alarmed at my use of the word Commonwealth.[51] The Commonwealth is that social state in which God and Nature meant us to live. Ireland will yet be a Commonwealth of Commonwealths; a Nation of many nations, and every Nation a Commune.

I find I have still some things to say, especially concerning the meaning of this much misunderstood word, the "Commune".[52]

FURTHER CONTRIBUTIONS
TO *THE IRISH WORKER.*
DECEMBER 1912–MAY 1913

The Irish Worker, Christmas Number, 1912, p.1, cols. 1–3; p. 2, cols. 1–3

HEROES AND THE HEROIC:
AN ADDRESS TO YOUNG IRELAND.

Conventionally we speak of the Heroic Period as that which witnessed the emergence and mighty exploits of the Red Branch of Ulster and their gigantic contemporaries of Ulster and their gigantic contemporaries in the other Provinces; but really the Heroic Age never ends. There are always heroes and the heroic; otherwise mankind would die out and leave the earth empty. Wherever that which is good and right and brave and true is loved and followed, and that which is base despised in spite of its apparent profitableness, there the heroic is present. The heroic is not something to talk about, make books about, write poetry about, but something to be put into act and lived out bravely. And I write so because of late years I notice a growing tendency on the part of our young people to talk grandiloquently about the Heroes of Ireland while they themselves, and quite deliberately, lead most unheroic lives.

The Heroic has been here always ever since the Celt first set foot in Ireland, mostly indeed unremembered and uncelebrated, but from time to time shining out resplendently and memorably in certain great classes and orders of Irish mankind. Consider these various famous orders which have exhibited the heroic temper and observe their most notable characteristics.

First came the super-human and semi-divine Heroes of "The Heroic Period", conventionally so called. They were really the children of the gods of our Pagan forefathers, and their story, which has been very much rationalized by the historians, belongs rather to the world of literature and imagination than to that of actual fact.

The young Red Branch Heroes were educated in the open air and the light. There they learned to shoot javelins straight at a mark, the care of horses, their training, the management of the war chariot, and chariot steeds, the art of the charioteer, the use of the sling; practised running, practised swimming in lake, river, or the sea, and grew up and lived men of the light, of the air, and of the field.

War and the preparation for war are distinctly and always open air occupations; and that is one of the reasons—it is the physical reason—why warlike nations and warlike aristocracies have been, on the whole so successful and enduring. True, war is murder, and murder is always murder, always a breach of one of Nature's great laws. But there is a greater law than this merely negative one, "Thou shalt not kill". There is its positive counterpart, "Thou shalt live and be a living cause of life," and this command cannot be obeyed by nations who spend the bright day within doors. Life and light and air are inseparable.

So, Peace is eternally good: "Blessed are the peace makers." But the peaceful must be men who are alive and well, not men who are corrupting. Therefore, when a Nation cries "Pax! Pax! war is horrible", and goes indoors, it is not long for this world.

What nation will be the first to preach and proclaim universal peace, declare the devilishness of murder? Not the nation that flees from the sun and wind, and goes indoors and sits at a desk crying Pax! Pax.

Those "beautiful feet upon the mountains"[53] will never be seen by the warrior nation, much less by the nation that goes indoors and sits at a desk and makes money—for a while.

The Red Branch were warriors, and, as such, men of the open air and the light, their lives spent in grand physical activities out of doors.

Finn and the Fianna Eireen come next in the grand roll of our heroic orders. They were essentially not so much warriors as hunters, and, as such, familiar with field and forest, rivers and lakes, mountains and the sea. They lived in the open air and the light, lived close to Nature and loved Nature well.

Said Finn:—

"I love to hear the cry of the hounds let loose from Glen Rah with their faces out from the Suir, the noise of wild swine in the woods of Mullaghmast, the song of the blackbird of letter lee, the thunder of billows against the cliffs of Eyrees, the screaming of sea gulls, the wash of water against the sides of my ship, the shouting of Oscar and the baying of Bran early in the morning," &c., &c.[54]

They lived in the open air, and loved well all the sights and sounds of nature.

Let them pass; men of the light and the air, diffusing from their memory after two thousand years, from their very names a gracious odour, "the smell of the field which the Lord hath blessed".[55]

The next grand order of heroic Irishmen, though not hitherto thought of in that light, were the founders of the great monastic communities conventionally known as "the Saints". These men are absolutely historic and just as real and actual as ourselves. Also they were Heroes, and the greatest in that kind probably that ever appeared anywhere on the earth's surface to that date. They were born aristocrats, warriors, lords of the land and owners of slaves, into whose souls there flashed miraculously the great eternal truth that man ought not to live upon the labours and sufferings and degradation of other people, but that, and especially while young and strong, he ought to sustain himself and others, too, by the labour of his own divine hands. Consider that. And so the Hero-Saints of Ireland, kings and sons of kings, great chieftains and great chieftains sons and near kinsmen, lords of land and exactors of tributes and masters of working slaves went forth and ploughed the earth and sowed it and reaped it, and dug drains through marshes and reclaimed wildernesses, and made good roads, and planted orchards and gardens, and tended flocks and herds and bees, and built houses and mills and ships, and became weavers and carpenters and shoemakers, and converted waste places into paradises of peace and plenty. For, presently their magazines were overflowing with wealth, wealth which was of their own creation, not bought or acquired by violence, wealth which they scattered freely to all that were in need and to all travellers and visitors, extending to all a limitless and glad hospitality.

Why did those great men and women and secular princes and princesses, scions of a proud and powerful and martial aristocracy, undertake this slaves' work and with such pride and joy? Mainly because they were already proud and brave men, noble and beautiful-souled women, and filled already with a certain heroic ardour. Then as Christians, too, they remembered who it was whom they worshipped and what was His life. So the eternal truth flashed in upon their souls with a blinding glory, blinding them to everything but itself. Has universal History anything to show us like the lives of those early Irish Christians? And so they passed, and our foolish mankind began to make gods and goddesses of them,[56] and to tell silly stories about them, and Ireland's punishment to-day for all that folly is that men are more inclined to laugh at the Saints than to imitate them, and anti-Irish historians like Froude[57] are able to tell us that we Irish have had no historical celebrities at all, only "a few grotesque saints"!

As they pass those Hero-Saints Irish imitators of their Divine Lord, we see again the re-emergence of the old Pagan-Heroic Ideal in our mediaeval chieftainry and their martial clansmen, an Ideal whose realization involved necessarily violence, rapine in many forms, the war cult, the worship of the sword. Let them pass, too, however great and brave. They had at least a Pagan-Heroic Ideal which they bravely followed and in which they honestly believed. Have you any Heroic Ideal, Pagan or Christian, which you believe in as honestly and follow as bravely? The Irish chieftainry and their martial clansmen were essentially warriors, and as such men of the open air and the light.

Next emerge the Protestant Irish landed gentry of Ireland of the eighteenth century. Children of the English Conquest, the gentlemen of Ireland, successors of the defeated chieftains, men whose right to be included in our heroical types and orders will be disputed by no one who remembers that grand heroic spirit exhibited by those settlers and colonists, when, in 1782, in the face of an angry Empire, they put forth their famous and unforgettable "Declaration of Irish Independence", standing in arms, determined and defiant behind their Declaration. Their faults and follies which have been punished by the extreme penalty of extermination will be forgiven or ignored by History,[58] which will remember only that one grand historic act of theirs and the noble spirit from which it sprung [*sic*]. They were not city gentlemen, but country gentlemen; essentially men of the open air and the light.

Finally, and for the first time, emerged into visible influence and power a great class and order of Irishmen here always, though concealed, from the beginning, and which will be here to the end, the Irish peasantry, the men of the plough and spade, tillers of the earth and tenders of cattle, a great order always as the strong foundation of all other classes and interests whose grand peasant virtues and strength, derived from the Earth, the Sunlight, and the Air, need no celebration by me.

Now, all these heroic types and orders of Irish manhood from the Red Branch to the Peasant of to-day have been open-air men, men who drew into themselves the strength of the earth and the life-giving force of the sunlight and the pure air, and who lived in close and vital touch with nature, familiar with field and forest and stream, with the plains and hill sides of Ireland. They all led their lives mainly in the open air, which were also lives of strong physical activity in the open air. Such were the Red Branch, and the Fianna of Finn and the Hero-Saints of the sixth and seventh centuries and the chieftainry and the gentlemen of the eighteenth century.

The History of Ireland is the History of its heroic types and orders,[59] and the heroic, as our History teaches us, whatever else it may be, is something which is begotten in the open air and cherished there by the great elemental forces of Nature, and fed and sustained mainly by physical activity in the open air.

You who live contentedly within doors and found your lives, such as they are, upon unmanly effeminate occupations, nursed within doors, ought not, save as an honest preparation for action,[60] presume to talk or write at all about Heroes and the Heroic or about Irish History which, in essence, is nothing else than the history of our heroic types and orders.

Now, the Saints, according as their primal fire burned low, began to sneak into their cloisters and libraries out of the light, and to live on the labours of serfs; and the gentlemen of Ireland, our landlord order, according as they, too, failed and their natural force abated, retreated into cities, town houses, villa residencies and clubs.

To-day our peasantry aim their best thither also, that is city-wards, and, as they can't get there, send thither their scions, their boys and girls; held and governed as they are by the huge superstition of our time that it is a grand thing to have money and live without labour on the labour of others. And, it is not a grand thing at all but a very mean and vile, and, as an ideal, nothing else than "a blasphemous fable and a damnable deceit".[61]

Now, all these Heroic types fall short of the Ideal, the Ideal which this century and our time present to us. The Red Branch and the Fianna were men of blood. They are not for us; save with reservations.

The brave chieftainry and their clansmen were, too, men of blood. They, too, are not for us; save with reservations.

The landed gentry lived without labour on the labour of others. They are not for us.

The Hero-Saints, save and except that we cannot be all celibates, are for ever and for us all a grand pattern exemplar and realized ideal. They lived mainly in the open air and the light working there with their hands at noble and useful and beautiful occupations. Otherwise they worked indoors in their workshops, and on such manly labour outdoor and indoor they erected their great spiritual, intellectual, scholarly, and artistic life. None of the other heroical types are for our imitation, save with great reservations. The Hero-Saints are.

They saw that war was wrong, infernal, contrary to Christ's law: they gave their swords to the smiths to be beaten into spades and hatchets. They saw that slavery was wrong infernal, contrary to Christ's law. They flung away their whips and freed their slaves, and did their own work. So they became great, famous and powerful. Theirs was the greatest effort made in all time to overthrow the dominion of the evil Power which holds mankind in thrall.

They could not conquer, annex and absorb the world, nor did they ever intend to, or even hope to. Their vows of celibacy kept them also a distinct order, and even a small order.

The Peasant labours as the Saints laboured; but he labours under compulsion, not freely and joyfully; and he works selfishly, with an eye to the main chance. He does not believe in his own great life.

The Heroic ideal of our century, of man to-day involves (1) life in the open air and the light; therefore in the country; (2) a life founded upon the useful physical activities; that is to say labour. Observe, I do not say consisting of such activities but founded upon them, as the spirituality and intellectuality, the art and the scholarship of the saints had their base and foundation in such activities. (3) Labour not devoted to money-making, but to the creation and promotion of life and all that makes life worth living.

If you have this Ideal in your souls, if you hold it and believe in it as firmly and absolutely as you hold and are convinced that money is a good thing, you will discover, without any prompting from me or another, the ways and means of reducing the Ideal into practice. Believe in anything with all your whole heart and the difficulties in the way of its realization melt away like mists before the rising sun.

Think of that life and compare it with the vile effeminate unheroic life to which the world, and for its own purposes, is inviting you to-day. It draws you into its many well-baited and alluring traps, and kills you there after a while and after it has squeezed out of you all it wants.

The Heroic Ideal of our century, of a time when no young man of understanding can believe any more in stealing, robbing, and killing, can be no other than that of our Irish Hero-Saints only, leading some such manly open-air life. You must fall in line, and marry, and multiply, and replenish the Earth.

Armed with this faith, nothing can stop you, nor can any limits be assigned to your advance.

The practical outcome of our historical review is this: If you desire to lead a brave and manly life, you will in one way or another, probably by purchase, secure possession of a sufficient area of your native land, and there create a self-maintained society, founded upon those manly physical creative activities which are exerted mainly in the open air and the light. If you determine to do that, everything that lives will be on your side. God and Nature and Man will help you; Sun and Wind, and Earth, and Water will co-operate with you and be your friends and allies. Such a Society will be a Nation, and such a Nation the whole world will not be able to put down and will not want to put down.

The Irish Worker, 1 February 1913, p. 3, cols. 4–5.

ADDRESS TO LABOUR LEADERS.
(CONTINUED.)

Congratulations on late successes.[62] I hope you will capture Municipal Dublin, ward by ward, and begin the Herculean task by cleansing this huge congested city, bringing out its massed poor people into the adjoining country, bringing in light and air, and, at the same time, relieving the congestion, mitigating the unemployment, and reducing the intolerable rents.

If you were in power you could do all this; but you are not, and no enthusiasm or expenditure of energy and enthusiasm will hasten the Ward elections. Also mighty influences are against you, and will probably mass themselves and combine once your object is clearly seen, and the vested interests now vaguely apprehensive become seriously alarmed.

Then meantime little children pine and perish, young hearts and heads are growing grey, bright eyes are fading; hope, faith, enthusiasm, and expectation are yielding to disappointment and care.

But I am not here, coming unbidden into what is the Forum or Council Chamber of Irish Labour, to offer empty congratulations or an idle sympathy to those remoter aims and purposes which you understand better than I do. I am here to urge you, all I can, into instant action for the salvation of the overthrown and defeated, and especially of the children, nine-tenths of whom are without proper nutrition. I want you to interpose your giant strength between the condemned and their execution, forgetting, if for a moment, your own wrongs, however great and flagrant, and to do it at once; begin to do it without an instant's unnecessary delay. For I perceive that you can; also that in doing it you will assume the virtual command of this great city, Ireland's capital, and without the attachment of a single cross on a voting paper.[63] I see that you lack nothing for that work—a work which only seems to be gigantic; and if it is gigantic, are not your resources gigantic, too? On your side I see powerful combinations of employed working people solid in their unions and loyal to their leaders. A vast unorganized, but nobly idealistic, urban democracy, chafing at their condition, righteously indignant; vast rich and waste lands within rifle shot of your headquarters, and, in your total collective strength, incalculable financial resources. Only rekindle the quenched fire of Faith in the heart of the people; make them feel that, contrary to what seems, God and man have actually not deserted them; send down but one ray of Hope into their dim habitations, and things will follow even from the moment that you issue your proclamation and declare your purpose.[64]

Man is so constituted that he can almost live upon Hope, while, without hope, he will die, even with millions to his credit in the bank. A famous warrior once invaded Italy. He led a great army, but his war chest was ill furnished. The tribunes and centurions and delegates of the legions of the army met in public assembly, and passed a resolution, and sent it to their General. "General", they said, "You can take all our pay for your war chest, and for as long as you please. All that we want is bread and iron."

That was for war, conquest, violence, devastation, the manning and slaying of myriads of men like themselves. Men are the same now as they ever were. They can live upon Hope and a crust. Stir a spirit like that in the heart of your people and victory is assured.

If you could but shift one hundred families, to begin with, out into the pure, wholesome, food-producing country, vacating thereby at once a hundred dingy habitations, it would make at least some impression upon rent, upon employment, upon the very low standard of wages, upon the prevailing destitutions.

I assume that you would have all these people employed and producing more, far more than the cost of their maintenance. That is the grand central fact of the situation in our times. The most unpromising workers, children as well as old people, if they only get fair play, will produce wealth in vast masses. Such is the immense productivity of labour in our time, assisted as it is by such labour-saving contrivances as were never even dreamed of before.

But when you begin to bring the people out, by the thousand at the time, you have Dublin at your feet, and the social revolution begun without the firing of a shot. Nor will you thereby seriously antagonize any vested interests, as I hope to show in a later paper.

Meantime, fix your mind upon this the astonishing, the miraculous productivity of labour in this new and strange time of ours. In this connection buy and read Captain Petavel's "The Coming Triumph of Christian Civilisation" (Allen & Co., London, price 1s).[65]

The great productivity of human labour, properly equipped—with the ways and means of production—it is not a phrase at all; it is a fact.

I have two young friends in Canada who between them plough, harrow, sow, and harvest 640 acres of land. They have each a team of eight horses, drawing an eight-shared plough, with seats on which they sit and drive. There is a harrow attached, so that ploughing and harrowing are one operation. They grow some 12,800 bushels of wheat per annum to supply the world with bread. They lead hard, bare, lonely lives, far from home and friends and all the refinements of civilization. They have not made their fortunes yet, nor are like to make them, for the exploiter is as busy there as here, duly reappearing in every new land. The devil went over to America in the "Mayflower".[66]

These young men—a fact to which I would ask your earnest attention—are anxious to get into the "real estate" business; that is, to capture the earth and become exploiters themselves. We are all guilty, in thought or in act, of the same great crime against humanity, all willing, ready, and anxious to be exploiters ourselves. Hate the crime, therefore, not the criminal; for if you hate the criminal you hate civilised mankind, and your own selves also.

And what I want you to do, if even on a small scale at first, is to create here in our own grand country, in relief of Dublin congestion and destitution and the fierce prevailing competition, to create here a small world, your own, where there will be no exploitation at all. Exclude out that one great crime, and imagination can hardly embrace the results, calculated only in material wealth.

(TO BE CONTINUED.)

The Irish Worker, 8 February 1913, p. 2, cols. 4–5.

ADDRESS TO LABOUR LEADERS.
(CONTINUED.)

A little world your own, no matter how small, from which exploitation is absolutely excluded. That means, if you will think the matter out, from which sweating, from which production for profit, profit-making, from which usury (interest dividends) from which forced labour, covetousness and overreaching of man by man are excluded. Exclude but one of these things and you exclude all. Exclude usury alone and you exclude every other kind of gross tyranny and oppression, for, without usury in some form, man cannot prey upon man.

And therefore Moses, the greatest of all statesmen and law makers, when he was fashioning his people in the wilderness after the great Trek, delivered a most solemn interdiction of its practice.

> "Thou shalt not lend to thy brother in usury, usury of land, usury of money, usury of food, usury of anything that is lent upon usury."[67]

I say that the world is rotten with usury. Then I say in order to conquer the world you must go outside of it; you must establish outside of it a human society in which there shall be no usury, none whatever, of any kind or form.

Don't you know that this world of man in which you live is rotten with usury? It is so steeped, saturated, poisoned in every fibre with usury that usury governs you, even against your will. The great English Trade Unions have some eight millions of saved capital. It is mostly out at usury, invested in exploiting and profit-making businesses.

Yet, only 100 acres, 100 acres to begin with. From that scantling of Irish land exclude usury, profit-making exploitation. Let all the human activities there be directed only upon production for use, consumption and enjoyment, not for markets, and the results will astonish you.

All the natural easy and inviting inclines seem to lead you in that direction. You have an urban headquarters, Liberty Hall, for which you pay a huge rent; for the ground rents of Dublin are awful. I once made inquiries into that subject. Why not have also a rural headquarters, a group of bungalow buildings, but with 100 acres attached, all your own, and establish here, cause to reign here that spirit of liberty, equality and fraternity which will animate those greater socialistic republics of which you dream. This small thing is in your power, those other great things are not. Then that group of bungalow buildings might be erected largely by the volunteered labour of the young Dublin democracy. Now, if you had on the land 500 of the 2,000 poor children, and 100 of the 500 sandwich men whom you entertained last Christmas, and working under skilled direction, might they not do much to enable you to entertain great numbers of happy holiday-making people coming out on Saturdays and Sundays to their own lands and their own rural headquarters. I can only here give a hint or suggestion of the line of action which I should like to see you adopt.

To return to the lads whom I left tilling 640 acres of land in Canada. If you had these two young Irish-Canadians working here at potato-culture as there on wheat-growing, what amount of this staple food would they supply year by year to your store houses? Seemingly, 6,400 tons, at the rate of 10 tons to the acre. Ten tons an acre is, indeed, a little above the average which for our old-fashioned farming is about 8. But as you will not stint them in seeds, fertilizers, or in any direction, I assume that their culture will also be above the average, and I know that good farmers grow even more than 10 tons to the acre.

Think of the 16 bags of coal which go to make a ton of coal; it will help you to imagine what a ton of potatoes actually means. Many people don't know the meaning of our large weights and measures. I had to look up the concrete significance of a bushel in writing this address—it means 64 pints. If these lads were growing for you Irish wheat or barley at the rate of 50 bushels an acre the outcome of their year's work would be more than two millions of pints!

You will remember I mentioned an English firm which last year, 1912, grew 72 bushels from a single acre. You will say those Canadian lands need no annual manuring. That is so; but there are now machines which spread out manure more evenly, and ten times more quickly, than it could be done by fork and hand. Then, with such ploughs, those potatoes might be plowed out in a few days, and gathered, brought home, and stored joyfully by hundreds of happy children in ox carts and donkey carts. Imagine that harvest morning—the bands and banners and the shouting. We are somewhat removed as yet from the realization of such things; but such things will be. Children, like grown-ups, have got to be emancipated. In these papers I am addressing your imagination, indeed, your sense of what might be, ought to be, will be; but in doing so always endeavour to bring along with me your reason, understanding, and knowledge derived from experience. But I know well that unless in some way I affect your imagination, I can do nothing. Without imagination the thought, picture, or mental presentation of what the world will be when the power of usury is overthrown, I would not be writing these words. Without imagination all action is impossible; without it man is as helpless as a sailing ship without wind. What makes you Socialists? What leads you to strike? What chains the working millionaire to his desk? Imagination. It is the driving force of the world.

Imagine now, if only to please me, that you control an agricultural and industrial estate in the country, consisting of 10,000 acres. It is only a small part of our noble country; also that you have here, and busily and gladly employed, 10,000 people, brought out from the congested slums and streets of Dublin. Think of the fall of rents which would follow such an exodus, of the reduction of unemployment, the advance of wages, the improvement of conditions.

To what extent would the labours of those two young men, assisted by the children, meet the requirements of such a "garden city", planted out there, and well furnished otherwise with an abundance of the necessaries of life?

Ten thousand people all told—infants, children, boys and girls, and grown-ups and aged—will consist of about 2,000 families and homes. A family will need, on an average, two stones of potatoes for the week, or 104 for the year. Multiply 2,000 by 104, and the product, 408,000 stones, represents the quantity of potatoes required by this population of 10,000. Now, reduce the stones to tons, and you find the result—2,550 tons. But these lads, well equipped with land, fertilisers, the best seed, with horse power and mechanical power, will produce some 6,400 tons; that is, a great deal more than twice as much as is necessary.

I don't think I am overstating what those lads could do, observed, too, as they would be, by ten thousand pairs of eyes, many of them female; criticised, blamed, praised and applauded, by near 10,000 persons depending upon them for the filling of their magazines, for the provision of this necessary of life, the ever-welcome, wholesome, delicious, and well-flavoured potato. But, if I have made an overstatement, there is a good deal to draw upon in the way of deduction. There is the difference between the 2,550 tons required by the agricultural and industrial garden city and the 6,400 tons which, at the rate of 10 tons to the acre, I am assuming that these lads will be able to grow.

(TO BE CONTINUED.)

The Irish Worker, 15 February 1913, p. 4, cols. 3–4.

ADDRESS TO LABOUR LEADERS.
(CONTINUED.)

Remember, too, that the petrol-driven plough is already coming into action. In an agricultural paper I have just been reading of one such, provided with a double share, on which a man sits and guides—will not an old man do here as well as a young?—and which will plough three acres a day. The cost is, I think, £75. The plough can be detached from the mechanism, which will then work other labour-saving contrivances as well. We are only in the beginning of the agricultural revolution—a revolution of which I want you to be the masters, not the slaves and victims. Horses need much care, much food, a great deal of bedding, and extensive stabling accommodation. Petrol-driven machines need only a little care and a little oil, and are not liable to—glanders. My young Canadian friends, some time since, lost all their horses. The enlightened Canadian Government, which can spare seven millions for Dreadnaughts,[68] gave them no compensation, mere labour being as much victimised in new lands as in old.

Now, how much do you working people pay over the counter for 6,400 tons of potatoes bought at 8*d.* a stone? More than £34,000 for what our two young men produce by some two months of pleasant labour. Such are hundreds of horseleeches of exploiters who fasten themselves on to every kind and form of wealth, even the plainest necessaries, from the moment of their inception to the time when they are bought and consumed.

Even at a great cost it would pay you well to buy the means of production, and to produce not for gain, but for use, consumption, and enjoyment.

A social system founded upon exploitation implies also an incredible amount of most wicked waste. Now, beat round the whole compass of things that minister to the pleasures and amenities of a bright and happy life and you will find that they may all be produced by an astonishingly small amount of labour—food, clothes, houses, furniture, etc.—labour which to our young, active, happy, and high-spirited people will be the merest bagatelle; labour which, being unforced and free, volunteered, will be a continuous delight; not, as most labour is to-day, a grind and a bore.

Free labour and labour free will do deeds of which we can hardly form a conception to-day where labour is driven to its work like a slave.

"Drain the Bog of Allen?"

Yes, reclaim the Sahara.

Unbind Prometheus. Too long has the Titan been chained; too long have countless vultures been tearing at his entrails.

And you will not do it by violence—by the violence of strikes or the violence of State-made laws.

"Blessed are the peacemakers." It is as true to-day as it was two thousand years ago.

In America boys under fourteen have, as I learn from an American paper, already beaten all records in the quantity and quality of wheat raised from a given area. Girls have done the same feat in tomato culture—broken all records. In 1912 boys all but broke the record in tomato culture, raising as many as 840 bushels to the acre. I confess I don't know the capacity of the American bushel; but the boys evidently did great things.

Then might not an intelligent active boy of 14 or 15 sit and guide a petrol-driven plough or some such other labour-saving contrivance, so exempting men for noblier [sic] and manlier activities?

I have noticed already the astonishing productivity of child labour in horticulture quoting a passage from the American

State Papers, let me re-quote it:—

"By putting in a new crop as soon as was harvested, school garden boys, 11 to 12 years old, raised on a sixteenth of an acre, 336 bunches of radishes, 110 bunches of onions, 368 heads of lettuce, 89 bunches of beets, 8 bushels of beans, 7 bushels of tomatoes, 7 bunches of carrots, 1 peck of turnips, besides nasturtiums and petunias, many boxes of which found their way to the hospitals of the city. This was at Washington, on the grounds of the Department of Agriculture."

Surely in our children we have a mighty river of potential Irish wealth now running to waste.

Is it not very possible, more than possible, probable, that those small nimble hands, directed by active and docile minds, might almost support us all if only well and wisely directed? They surely would, if to the children we add boys and girls up to the age of 16.

I imagine all adult labour free, free and directed out upon the world for the undertaking of great enterprises.

If I could put all that I have to say into one word that word would be—TREK!

In the early times of the Republic the people of Rome, being oppressed intolerably by an exploiting and usurious Patriciate, determined neither to fight their oppressors nor to remain out of Rome, took up a position at a point where the Anio fell into the Tiber, and thence sent a herald to their late lords declaring that they had abandoned Rome for ever and that they were about to build a new city and be free. The Patricians, terrified at that prospect, granted all, and more than all, the demands of the people, who immediately returned. The reconciliation was complete and the infant Republic resumed her career—a career which was to end only with the conquest of the world.

That revolted and seceding Roman democracy would not imbrue their hands in the blood of those who had been their captains in war and leaders and guides in peace even though they had been cruel and tyrannical. Neither did they seize the lands of their lords. They chose as the site of their new city a territory which was sacred to the gods, believing that their cause was one of which the gods would approve.

The Patriciate, too, acted well on that occasion, refusing to wage war upon the seceders and making to them very great concessions.[69]

On both sides was shown a spirit worthy of a people destined to become the masters of the world. We are living to-day under influences of a hundred kinds emanating from the genius of Rome, and Rome began in that grand trek and the resulting grand reconciliation when sprang internal cohesion and external warlike power.

I read with great interest "Shellback's"[70] suggestion as to the camp for our working people during the summer and autumn months. Such an institution, once actually realised, might grow and expand rapidly, and in most promising directions. The golfers have their golfing grounds, and many of the clerks of Dublin have camps here and there in the country. If our manual workers move out in this direction, too, it might prove a starting point for the achievement of great things. It certainly will, if well led. The great democracy of Dublin will never be a handful of the better-paid clerks. The movement, well initiated, is bound to go far.

I just throw out the following ideas for your wider consideration. I feel on sure ground when dealing with principles, but am very diffident when trying to apply principles in action.

It should be easy, no doubt, to hire a camping field, hire tents; but how to deal practically, without great prior preparation, with thousands—tens of thousands—of people moving thither, and expecting to have a good time—that is, indeed, a matter needing the management of robust geniuses, masters and mistresses of organisation. Then, if you charge the visitors and campers, those most in need of light and air, rest and change, won't be able to pay. If you don't charge, the expense will be tremendous. Now, people will pour out money lavishly for a great idea, but I don't think they will, only to let the working people have a run in the country as the North of England people take a summer run to the Isle of Man. Like an Isle of Man trip the thing would end in itself.

I suggest an early, an immediate purchase or permanent hiring of a tract of land, say, to begin with, 100 acres, out in the country, a rude equipment of the same, to start with; the transference thither, with caretakers, teachers, and instructors, of 1,000 of our children, or as great a number of our children as possible, and of as many of our unemployed people as possible, all under the control of one competent person, either Miss Larkin[71] herself or someone whom she might choose. This one person ought to be assisted by a small committee.

The unemployed and the children, all under due instruction and proper control, and all well fed and cared for from the start, would begin at once to make all the preparations necessary for the advent of the working population of Dublin in the summer and autumn months. There would be all the spring and early summer for these preparations, so that, when the great outward movement of the people takes place, all the main contingencies would be both foreseen and provided for—tents, rough temporary shelters, cooking arrangements, eating rooms, concert and lecture halls, sanitary arrangements, the water supply, and an abundance of plain, wholesome food, given freely to all, such as milk, butter, oatmeal porridge, vegetables, potatoes, bread and cakes, and plain pudding, well served, too, with all the amenities and refinements of the best side of our civilisation, the children, neatly and prettily dressed, doing all the attendance, having been taught to serve and attend, and to serve the poorest with as much consideration and submissiveness as they would the richest.

Not a great deal can be one in the first year; but all that I have suggested is perfectly feasible.

The Irish Worker, 22 February 1913, p. 3, cols. 1–5.

ADDRESS TO LABOUR LEADERS.
(CONTINUED.)

I say perfectly feasible, because, though I may be charged with tiresome reiteration, I would press upon your notice the astonishing—the incredible productivity of well-directed labour. So great is it that even children and old people and "unemployables", the very cripples and the blind may, without working a degree too hard or an hour too long, create wealth in vast masses, that is things necessary or desirable for all the rational purposes of human life. "Unemployables" are only persons out of whom Capitalism does not expect to make gain. Yet an "unemployable" old woman might very well care for six children, or manage 100 poultry, or knit 300 pairs of stockings in a year. No one is unemployable except the dead. And even they—. Don't the dead preach?

Once you buy the land, and the people know that it is their very own, and going to be used for great popular purposes, they will go out in numbers on Saturdays and Sundays, and surely will take off their coats while there, and, in obedience to instruction and direction, do a vast amount of cheerful volunteered work. The work done so, and the expenditure of money saved so, are obviously incalculable; all depending on the people's spirit and loyalty, and the numbers crowding thither for week ends during the Spring months. If you can kindle the imagination of the people all will go well; if not—well, it is hard to make a fire out of wet sticks. However, the sticks are not, in my opinion, wet at all but very dry and inflammable if you only bring and apply the fire.

Let us consider the probable expenses of making a start. The cost of a holding of 100 acres—that is of the price of the tenant's good will—would be from £1,000 to £1,500—say £1,250. Land is dearer according to proximity to a railway.

I mention 100 acres so that you may see how things might work out. Of course you might buy one of 70 acres or 120, or you might not buy but rent.

For the equipment of the estate let us put down £2,750; total, £4,000. It looks a large sum for working people, but, really, if you can only get the people to understand and sympathise, a far larger sum than this would be nothing to them; such is the mighty power of numbers. Is it not from their pennies and sixpences that the adulterators of food make such great and base profits.

I suggest that you, their known and trusted leaders, should get your own people first, those who are already strongly combined in the Unions, to agree in support of the movement and undertake to answer a whip for that purpose, one which would represent at least the purchase money, £1,250.

I assume, for I write somewhat in the dark here, that there are in and round Dublin some 50,000 persons, men and women, lads and girls, who are in Unions, and would respond to such an appeal if it is made by their own executives. A whip of 6*d.* or of 3*d.* paid in two successive weeks, would bring in £1,250, the approximate price of the land, leaving £2,750 to be supplied by the general public and the unorganised working classes through appointed collectors and also at public meetings where the nature and meaning of the movement would be explained. I am myself a wretched public speaker and dislike public exposure; but, if you think I might be of some service, would make an attempt or two, to express the faith that is in me.[72]

If the people show that they are in real earnest, and moving out in this matter on their own initiative, and relying upon themselves,[73] I am convinced that a very great and growing assistance will be forthcoming from the classes. Great causes—and surely this is a very great cause—are never left without material support. I have just learned that one of our religious minorities send out yearly near £50,000 for "the conversion of the heathen". The more impersonal and disinterested[74] you can keep this movement the more will material aids and helps and assistances flow towards it, presents and gifts of many kinds, even land or money to buy lands. You see I am only applying a great and universal principle when I say:—"Don't charge those summer guests. Give out freely everything that the estate is able to produce", and it can produce a great deal.

Also the classes are already very uneasy in their minds about the conditions of the Dublin poor. Their consciences are continually pricking them on the subject.

I put in a strong plea for rapid action, even at the cost of possible mistakes. During these spring weeks which are passing, one after another appearing and disappearing, we ought to be preparing the ground. We should be planting and sowing peas, beans, all manner of vegetables, sweet peas, too, and flowers for the brightening of tables, making preparation for the coming of the summer and autumn campers. We should have early potatoes and late potatoes. From ten tilled acres in the first year we might expect 80 tons of potatoes. Might not a thousand lads and men coming out from Dublin a fine weekend, Saturday afternoon and Sunday, and putting themselves under direction, negotiate rather successfully a great many acres, you supplying the hired horses and ploughs, tents, rude sleeping accommodation and simple fare? I should like to be in the camp that Saturday night listening to the music and the singing and the merry voices.

Of course, you will have no objection to Sunday activities. For this is sport, play, amusement; not servile labour.

Then, I assume that, from the moment of purchase, there will be a considerable number of men permanently attached, taken from the unemployed of Dublin, and growing stronger, bolder, and happier everyday, as well as more skilful and understanding.

Now, for the quickest-growing vegetables we would have to wait; but that grand and quite indispensable necessary milk could be provided for offhand. The children, at all events, will need milk from the moment of their arrival. You can buy milch cows at once; the children themselves will mind, care, and milk them always under instruction and direction. The ownership of her own cow would be a great reward to hold out for good behaviour to an ambitious little girl. They would soon grow fond of their cows, love them, and make them pets. Don't we see every day little girls entrusted with the care of homunculuses, that is, of men and women on a small scale?

A good milch cow costing £15 will give 50 pints of milk a day, and the cows will flourish on the rich and juicy herbage yielded everywhere by this fertile County of ours. Assuming, then, that the children will require an average of a pint a day, you would need ten cows at least for the children. Add ten more supplying for the grown-ups on the estate, for visitors and the campers when they come. The cost of the cows would be some £300, but they would be producing milk from the day of arrival. Indeed I would advise spending £1,000 straight off upon cows.

Then fields should be prepared and sown with oats and wheat, the weekend voluntary activity of young Dublin coming along to help, so that in the autumn the magazines should be full with an abundance of wheat, oats and potatoes, all your own, without the intervention and assistance of any gentleman of exploiting propensities.

You will see more and more clearly from day to day and month to month that while it is awfully hard to make money, and for working men and women impossible, it is very easy to create wealth, easy and also delightful. After a little of this kind of life your young people will despise football and wonder at the days when they went in their thousands and tens of thousands to see a ball kicked, and had to pay, too, for the privilege of witnessing that grand spectacle. For this is an eternal truth, that the Power which made us has made us to delight in labour, that is, in creative productive formative activities and of a thousand different kinds, each according to some natural bent given to him from or even before his birth.

I expect that many of the campers will be anxious to settle permanently on the Estate and lead a rural life, and that you will then be able to accommodate and maintain them and supply them with appropriate occupations.

I only regard that estate of 100 acres as a nucleus, continually growing and expanding. When the people understand what is forward and feel how good it is to have land of their own and feel in every fibre the thrill of freedom and the glow of good nature and kindly human relations you will experience no lack of funds. The 100 acres will soon grow to 1,000 and the 1,000 to 10,000.

Observe, too, that you might use the 100 acres as a starting point from which to annex, even this spring, many adjoining fields hired in conacre on the eleven months' system from the neighbouring graziers. The young men coming out on weekends, perhaps, in thousands, will not find enough to do on our small Estate; so you might hire those fields in conacre and let young Dublin expend its activities on those fields, with the result of thousands of tons of corn, potatoes, and food for the cattle.

For the direction of those agricultural activities I can think of no one better than Mr. Wibberley[75], now an organizer of the I.A.O.S. He seems to understand agriculture better than anyone else in Ireland. He is an enthusiast on the subject, too, and I am sure, with the consent of the I.A.O.S., could be got to supervise and direct. If unable to act himself, he could nominate a substitute on whom you could rely. For, of course, you must have a competent director of agriculture; competent directors, too, in all the departments of industry. But, at the beginning, agriculture is a thing of chief importance and the most pressing.

Personally I should like the first Camp to be pitched up Saggart way. Why? Well, the land here is very rich. Then the place is near the western Wicklow highlands, Kippure Shee Finn, Mullagh Clievaun, where the campers might spend delightful days mountaineering. They could bring tents with them from the Camp or sleep in the heather.

Also in this neighbourhood are extensive turf bogs now hardly gashed. There is one on the side of Ballinulta above Lacken, south-west of Blessington. The significance of this will be recognised if you remember that the Estate must, so far as possible, be self-sustaining. If you can cut, dry, and bring home turf there will be no coal bill. Now a few hundred merry lads and lasses camping for a couple of nights on the bog side will dig, turn over and stook a year's supply of fuel, which the children in their ox carts and donkey carts will bring home.

Also I look to see you taking in great tracts of this treeless western half of the great County, ring-fencing it and planting it. Armed with dynamite cartridges for the making of beds for the saplings, one man to-day can do as much as twenty men used to do having only spades for their digging instruments.

All this in due time. I want you to keep it in mind as a vista of progressive action, a great outlet, one of many, for the abounding activities of young Dublin, escaped if but for a fortnight from the yoke of wage slavery, full of life, energy, fire, and striking out towards the doing of great things.

What might not 500 children do well fed, well housed, breathing pure air, provided with the instruments and materials of production under kindly discipline and well guided and instructed? Give the boys tools and materials with a carpenter to govern the carpentry class, and they will make rough, sound, bedsteads, chairs, stools, tables, &c., in this ensuing April and May, enough for perhaps thousands of campers when they arrive.

In the production of useful and necessary things, and in almost every direction there is no difficulty at all. Only believe that there is no difficulty, and there is none.[76] All the wise saws and prudential maxims of our sordid civilisation don't apply here where nothing, nothing whatsoever, is done for profit. The old wisdom goes and the new comes, or rather craft and cunning go and wisdom comes. Now wisdom has much to do with the heart and not much with the head.

The campers will need tents, and tents are expensive even to hire, and I know from experience, dear and also bad. Get the canvas and ropes for the children, and they will make the tents and marquees, and the carpentry class turn out the tent pegs and the mallets. Next year you may be weaving your own canvas.

In a great many departments of industry active intelligent boys and girls are nearly as good as men and women. Perhaps better, being teachable, adaptable, and more willing to do as they are bid. There ought to be vast magazines of wealth in the hands, hearts, and brains of those children. I imagine you starting with 500 or 1,000 of them on the Estate.

The Campers should, I think, this year at all events, bring their own tea and coffee and meat, or do without these things, which, after all, are only luxuries. Whatever the Estate produces in abundance should be free to all. When you get to glass houses—the glass made on the Estate—there will be no shortage of tomatoes, grapes, and whatever is grown under glass. A few old men, assisted by a few children, will produce them by the ton; all in good time.

Meantime, [you will need] luxuries and scarce things for honoured elders and honoured invited guests like the Archbishops of Dublin, University professors, and the great Captains of industry, people accustomed to faring well, and who think it a little odd as guests to be set down to quite plain, if wholesome, fare.

Letter to Miss Delia Larkin. *The Irish Worker*, 8 March 1913, p. 4, col. 4.

> Braemar, Douglas Cross,
> Cork,
> 4th March, 1913.

DEAR MISS LARKIN,—I enclose the £5 I promised you with best hopes for your success. Use it JUST AS YOU THINK RIGHT; only I would like it spent primarily on children[,] unemployables, and unemployed, and on production for use, enjoyment, consumption, and not with any view to pecuniary results, exploitation, marketing; only just for the production of wealth—that is, of good things in as large quantities as possible. Get those "weak things of the world to confound the wise"[77] by the masses of plain wealth—plain first—that they are able to produce.

I should like the Trades Unions in their war with Capitalism to have land of their own, using it for war purposes; but this move of yours I would like you to keep OUTSIDE that zone of strife, and, so, a fit rallying-point for all who desire to help to solve the social problem without any fighting.

It is a poor little gift, nothing in comparison with what you need; but will be an indication to your friends and others of my earnestness.

> Yours sincerely,
>
> STANDISH O'GRADY.

The Irish Worker, 15 March 1913, p. 1, cols. 1–2.

TO OUR LABOUR LEADERS.
(CONTINUED.)

I ended my last by picturing you as the entertainers of Arch-Bishops and University Professors, Captains of Industry, and other great people who hardly think of you to-day, save as accessories and humble instruments of their own superior life and activity which they regard as the chief aim and end of the social state. I am imagining nothing not realisable, and even easily realisable. If your trekkers, led, guided, and inspired by you, fling themselves with our ancestral fire and élan upon the great work of the creation of wealth and refrain from all thought of the exploitation of the wealth which they produce[,] wealth you will have, and in overflowing abundance. Neither sell it like the covetous, nor hoard it like the rich fool. Scatter it. "There is that scattereth and yet increaseth."[78]

Revive that ancient and noble virtue of hospitality, a virtue which half redeems the blood-guiltiness of our war-loving Irish forbears. To-day who can practise hospitality? It needs money, and not one in a thousand of us has money enough for any kind of generous hospitality. The only thing we can do in that way is to "stand treat", a dubious and dangerous mode of satisfying a deep and noble human instinct, the instinct which prompts us to welcome others to a share of the good things which it is in our power to impart.

You, with your magazines, overflowing with plenty; you with large and spacious house accommodation which cost you nothing to provide only the glad labours of the building brigade, with your abundant ways, means, and resources, and your bright boys and girls for attendance—you might make us again as famous for this great virtue as we once were. You know the Venerable Bede has immortalised our hospitality in the ages when Ireland was the University of Europe, and had not yet learned the base, modern trick of selling knowledge, and making a gain out of the noble enthusiasms of young people searching passionately for wisdom.

Have your own guilds, friendly societies of scholars and savants and beat [*illegible words here*]. I say it seriously and with deliberation; because I know that you can do it; if you please. You are not; cannot well be, learned yourselves; but I trust you have not lost our traditional Irish love of learning. There is a beautiful Irish peasant poem describing the chief pleasures of the Blessed Virgin. The third pleasure arose for her:—

"When our Blessed Lord, her dear son, was able to read out of a book."

Nevertheless, no child should be forced to read. Let the child learn to read, if it likes; not otherwise. All this enforcement of the three R's is worse than vanity. It is a sin against childhood, a pollution of the sanctities of the young pure human soul.[79]

No one would to-day even dream of thrusting such sham-knowledge into the tender brains of little children, but that they think there is money in it, that it will enable the child to "get on", which, being translated, means money.

In your land of the free where money has no place, and want has no place, there also the love of money and the worship of money and the power of money will have no place.

From the start you will have your own doctors glad to serve you in return for a very generous maintenance and a very honourable position, and for the pleasure of practising their art.

Also, you will have your own clergyman no longer compelled by fierce necessity to walk half with God and half with Mammon. As you are aware, our religions have a very mundane side as well as a spiritual. They have their funds—must have them—and their funds are out at usury, therefore employed, like the funds in the Trades Unions, in the huge worldwide business of sweating and exploitation. This necessary materialism which has been thrust upon the spirituality draws away cruelly the sympathy of the ministers of Christ from the cause of Christ's poor to the cause of the Devil's rich, from the labouring suffering exploited many to the exploiting few.

Hence, in all countries, where civilization holds sway the working people, feeling profoundly that the religions, as practised, are against them, and on the side of their exploiters, are growing neglectful of religion altogether. The British working man does not go to church on Sundays. Generally, I believe, he lies in bed taking a good rest, and reading his favourite sporting paper.[80]

Now, those who turn against their religion have always had bad luck.

Therefore, have nothing at all to do with the growing irreligion of our times. Have your own clergymen, duly appointed by authority, with you. They will be free, free to walk the ways of their Master. Now, our religion is altogether on the side of the poor, has nothing at all to do with property, and is in irreconcilable, eternal war against exploiting property, is altogether on the side of man and everlastingly against man's enemy—that is, money.

I am as revolutionary minded as any of you, but I want a revolution of which Christ would approve, and over which the angels will rejoice, not one over which the devils will rejoice. And I see you all unconsciously—for you don't know the nature of the forces which are driving you—moving in this direction, moving towards a revolution which will be like the upbursting of all hell.

Now, I perceive that if you adopt that most ancient resource of all oppressed peoples, the Trek, and if you trek in the right spirit, leaving behind you usury and all that usury means, you will achieve a thousand times more than you possibly can do by the reddest of red revolutions, and that without entertaining an angry thought, or dealing a nasty blow, or sending a bullet into any poor human creature. Rich and poor, are we not all poor human creatures, all driven by the great demon who has us all in thrall?

The Irish Worker, 22 March 1913, p. 1, cols. 3–6.

TO OUR LABOUR LEADERS.
(CONTINUED.)

You are so accustomed ever since childhood to see wealth produced in such puny quantities and by such desperate and unintermitted labour that you necessarily experience a great difficulty in believing that it may be produced in illimitable masses by the glad labours of a few. And yet it is true; and, in a manner, I speak by the book.

In Bradford may be seen any day a little girl of fifteen tending a machine which weaves in one week as much cloth as in old times was woven by twenty expert men upon their handlooms in a whole month (see "A Day in a Woollen Mill").[81]

This little girl, therefore, so miraculously assisted, does day by day the work of 80 men. And this in a world where millions of people find it hard to get decent clothing!

Of course little girls ought not to be so employed at all; but that is another matter. I am treating now of the very small amount of labour necessary for the production of wealth in vast masses.

Now, a hand-loom weaver will, I understand, weave in one day cloth enough to make two suits of clothes. Suppose now that the little Bradford girl works 300 days in the year, for how many suits of men's clothes will she weave the necessary cloth? Multiply 80 by 300, and the result by 2. She will weave cloth enough for 48,000 suits of clothes.

I have already asked you to imagine a city of the new order founded in the country, and representing the first Trek out of Dublin, a city devoted to production, to the creation of wealth and not to the exploitation of wealth, and consisting of some 10,000 people. The men and lads here will be about 2,000. Will not such a little girl working such machinery supply them with all the cloth that they need? Surely; and also a gigantic surplus to be used for any purpose that you think right. That little girl could "clothe the naked" with a vengeance if she were appointed to do so.

Some one may here remark—"Even if that be so, you are evidently going too fast and too far. No doubt with such machineries it is easy enough to weave cloth in great quantities and with little human labour, but what about the wool? You write as if the wool came up spontaneously out of the ground ready to the weaver's hand."

Well, in a sense, and if you consider, you will find that to be so. Like all Nature's gifts the wool does come up, rather spontaneously out of the ground; out of the ground first, and then out of the sheeps' [*sic*] backs.

But, indeed, I have not forgotten the wool, nor the complex intricate machinery, nor the coal or oil necessary to drive it. All such things, without exception, come under the same universal law, which declares that though it is hard to make money, and for working people impossible, it is easy to create every kind of wealth.

As to the wool—let me tell an experience which once befell me. On the highlands above Glenmalure I met a friendly and communicative shepherd boy, who seemed glad to exchange a little human society for that of his dumb animals. Indeed, I perceived that the poor boy was desperately lonely: As we talked the sheep were scattered abroad over the mountain feeding. I noticed one lying down and drew his attention to her.

"She was never strong," he said, and gave me a sketch of her history from birth.

"Do you know all your sheep like that, one by one?"

"Every one of them," he said; "and I'd know every one of them if I had twice as many."

"How many have you?"

"Fifteen hundred."

"And you could take care of three thousand?"

"Just as well."

"May I ask what the owner pays you."

"Twelve pounds a year, clothes, and diet."

He complained of loneliness.

Thinking of Arcadian shepherds of old times, I advised him to get a flute and learn to play on it.

Now, as a fleece weighs about six pounds, here was a poor, ill-paid, lonely lad, cut off, save at night, from all human companionship, necessarily ignorant, and probably developing in his solitude some form of insanity. Yet this one lad grew yearly 9,000 pounds of wool; besides some 1,500 sheep, the natural increase of his flock, sent yearly from the mountains to market.

The boy got almost nothing for his labour, though by that labour he increased the world's wealth by 9,000 pounds of wool and 1,500 sheep every year.

When you take in great tracts of the Highlands of Wicklow your weaving and spinning machines will be in no lack of wool, nor will your brave shepherd lads there lack anything that loyal lads ought to have, including gratitude, appreciation, and honour.

No; there is no difficulty at all in the production of any and every kind of wealth; and as to the machineries, I dare say you could get boys from Wexford to start your workshops and teach your first classes the noble, interesting, and even fascinating art of working in iron.

And for ever within your sphere the odious devil's game of producing for lucre, and all manner of glorious possibilities instantly begin to reveal themselves.

I assume now that my shepherd boy was telling the truth when he said that he could care for three thousand sheep. Here then you have one lad who will never, never be rich, never enjoy a hundredth part of his fair share of the wealth he creates, producing yearly 18,000 pounds of wool and sending yearly to market 3,000 muttons.

Beat round the whole compass of things good and desirable, what I call wealth, and you will find the same law in operation everywhere, wealth produced with ease and in vast quantities, yet everywhere the producers of wealth held down and oppressed. Why? Because everything is exploited; everything is produced for markets for gain; everyone is mad after money. In the pursuit of this thing everyone is trampling down everyone else.

And it is all madness. Get outside of this mad world. Create a new world; begin to create a new world in which productions will be for use, consumption, enjoyment, and not for markets for exploitation.

And there is no external difficulty. The difficulty is in your own minds. You can't yet believe it possible to do such things; you can't yet even imagine yourselves outside the continual control of money, seeing all the life that surrounds you saturated with money steeped in it in every fibre.

As to the purchase of machinery, I make a suggestion, the adoption of which will, I think, save you many thousands of pounds.

The great manufacturers can only afford to keep in use the most perfected and up-to-date machinery. Everything that does not come up to that pitch they scrap. They must scrap if they wish to maintain their position against the deadly, world-wide competition to which they are subjected.[82]

Now, as you don't produce for gain, for markets, but for use, consumption, and enjoyment, such scrapped machinery, which you will get for a song, will amply meet all your needs. That Bradford weaving machine which does the work of eighty men superseded one which did, perhaps, the work of seventy. But if you have a little girl equipped with this latter wonderful bit of mechanism, and so turning out cloth enough in one day to provide suits of clothes for a hundred and forty persons, why need you bother because the Bradford man works machinery a degree more effective? You only want to provide raiment for the unclad or ill clad. You have escaped from the fierce necessity which is driving him, which makes him, not only the master and lord of those iron engines, but their slave.

Similarly in all departments of industrialism—shoemaking, spinning, toolmaking, etc., etc.—you can buy, almost for the price of the steel, miracles of mechanical ingenuity for which the mad, Mammon-driven world has no further use.

Then you can and will use such machineries quietly and at your leisure. Why should you be in a hurry? Why wear yourself out before your time with fret and fever? God is not in a hurry. Nature is not in a hurry. Why should you? Someone said, "It is vulgar to be in a hurry." I think it is. At all events one of the greatest, noblest, and most beautiful results of an industrial activity which aims only at production, and not at gain, is the consequent leisure, tranquillity, and peace of mind which it will enable you to enjoy. It will give you time for everything, and plenty of time.

I have more than once pictured your children as driving ox carts. I have several reasons for desiring to see that gentle beast return to his old and honoured place in our rural economy. He is inexpensive to keep, easy to govern, and will do with pleasure a great deal of useful haulage and conveyancing. Then you can trust him to the care of children; you can't trust children with horses. Also there is no animal so tranquil minded, therefore, none such a preacher of tranquillity.

Can you imagine a more pleasant sight than a train of carts drawn by oxen in shining harness, driven by happy, rosy-faced, brightly-dressed children, moving towards the Port of Dublin, everyone making way for them, and returning with their load of coal, iron, or whatever imported things you need for your growing and expanding centres of rural civilisation.[83]

I suppose you are aware that the ox was the first Christian. The ox and the ass worshipped the Infant Saviour before the advent both of the Shepherds and of the Wise Men from the East. The ox was the first Christian.

When I urge you to undertake that Trek out of Dublin into the country I am thinking not so much of the material abundance, of the overflowing wealth which will be the first consequence, as of the resulting quiet, tranquillity, and peace of mind. In that city where this our deadly competition has no place every one will have time for everything, and leisure will abound like wealth. Why should you be in a hurry when a tenth, a twentieth part of your available labour supply—and that free, glad, volunteered—will suffice for the supply of everything that you need, and of every kind of rational luxury, comfort, and convenience.

For you won't force, drive, or coerce your people to work. Has not poor humanity been forced and driven long enough, and with most sorry results? Try Freedom now, for a change. I am sure it will do you good. Then, if you determine to give the people their Freedom, don't measure it out with a salt spoon. Give the poor people a long, deep, full draught of it, holding under control only the children, the immature boys and girls, and the few poor people who suffer evidently from disturbances of mind.[84]

I hope most sincerely you will make a great effort to carry out this year, "Shellback's" most excellent idea of a general summer camping out of the working people of Dublin. If you can carry out the idea it will be a glorious holiday for the poor people. I feel sure, too, that the idea is one with which employers will sympathise,[85] and that they will co-operate with you towards its realisation, that is, a fortnight's holiday for all the working people, a modern Irish form of that ancient "Feast of the Tabernacles" of the Israelites,[86] a move into the country, begun, continued, and ended in a holiday spirit, that is in a spirit of good nature, good and universal willingness to please and be pleased. I don't know anything which would so tend to create in Dublin such a general feeling of solidarity, of common interests, and mutual good will.

I imagine one camp as the fixed and stationary nucleus, the centre of order, management and control, for a great number of transitory camplets scattered according as grounds can be secured by hire or otherwise. Then I think of that central camp as the germ out of which the first city of the new order may grow, a city founded upon agricultural and industrial activities, undertaken without any reference to markets, exploitation, or any such sordid names, and which your Dublin

democracy will support generously and with all their great
collective financial power.

If they subscribed only an average of 6*d*. a week, which
they easily could if their hearts were once touched and their
imaginations kindled, would it not mean a revenue of more
than £100,000 a year, an income with which you could
almost do anything?

As to sanitation of a camp of that kind, you know how
civilisation deals with its waste matter. Civilised mankind
pours its waste matter into the rivers and pollutes them. The
waste products of humanity should be committed to the earth,
which requires it, and not to God's pure streams and the pure
sea, which reject it. The natural law governing all this sphere
of things was given long ago by the greatest of all Lawgivers.
(See Deuteronomy c. xxiv vv. 12, 13, 14.)[87] On this matter I
think ex-soldiers, accustomed to the methods of sanitation
employed in camps, might with advantage be brought into
consultation.

Indeed, in the foundation of any settlement, camp or city,
old soldiers and old sailors of a good type would be a most
useful element, they are so handy and resourceful, and can
bring such good results out of limited and poor materials.

For example, an old soldier will teach how to make an
Aldershot oven.[88] I saw one once in a camp. It is a device by
which one little fire will keep twelve pots on the boil or
simmering, a most ingenious yet most simple contrivance.
Old sailors seem to be able to do almost anything.

And don't, for the sake of your own souls, for the sake of
the children, do anything so plainly wrong, unnatural, and
unlovely as the conversion of a beautiful stream into a drain.
Civilization, I know, does it; but, in almost everything, you
will be safest in doing the opposite of what civilization does.
For 50 miles below Liverpool the pure sea is fouled and
darkened with the pollutions of Lancashire. In the North of
England I once saw a river flowing through a lovely glen.
That river was shocking. It seemed a river on fire, like
Phlegethon,[89] which, as you know, is one of the seven rivers

of Hell. But, indeed, Mammon stops at nothing, and, as it murders men, women, and children for the sake of a little base gain, we need not be surprised that it should also pollute streams, finding such practices to be "an economy", a lessening of the cost of production.

Then the adoption of that natural method of dealing with all waste matter will enable you to plant your camps, towns, cities, of the new order in any part of the country.

Don't you see that there is something awfully wrong, unnatural, and barbarous in the employment of our streams and rivers as drains?

The Irish Worker, 29 March 1913, p. 1, cols. 3–5.

TO OUR LABOUR LEADERS.
(CONTINUED.)

There was an error in my reference to Deuteronomy last week. Instead of chap. xxiv, read chap. xxiii. You might with great advantage read all the beautiful, humane, divinely inspired laws contained in that noble book.

You will never reform the world from within, not by the most cunning worldly devices, such as co-operative societies, or by any, even the most powerful combinations of working men, pursuing purposes, political, social or economic. How can you? How can you, whose inmost thoughts, most intimate, secret longings and aspirations, revolve in ceaseless worship around the Demon God who has us all in his grip; you who cannot even imagine a life worth living apart from the delicious prospect of having "plenty of money". How, in the name of common sense, can you overthrow the Money Power? How can you by any possibility exorcise from the soul of man that unclean spirit which has its sanctuary in your own hearts? While this love is in your hearts in vain will you combine, in vain rage against the tyranny of Capitalism. Then you know that this love is there fixed and rooted, and fed from the very life-springs of your being. Is there one of you who would not be a capitalist himself to-morrow if you could?

I know that in this social state such a universal cupidity is inevitable, unavoidable. You simply can't help loving money, because it is to-day the only known way towards the attainment of a life worth living.

What follows? If you see and understand these things, what ought you to do? Plainly to create a social state in which money will not be able to hunt, drive, and deprave men as it hunts, drives, and depraves men to-day.

Then the creation—it must be the creation, for you have no model or exemplar to copy—the creation of such a social state is not only well within your power, but all the inclines seem to lead in that direction. It concerns your most immediate economic necessities, largely meeting even their universal craving—quite natural and proper, too, in its way—of your working people for more money, that is, for more life.

Establish in the country, anywhere, even one Camp of 10,000 people, drawn from our congested capitol, and note the immediate and certain relief. Such a trek, and even upon that small scale, means the unexpected surrender of some 2,000 tenements; therefore an immediate and a mighty fall of rents, also a strong encouragement to the poor people to insist upon lowered rents and larger accommodation. How can we expect nice girls to emerge out of tenements where whole families, often with lodgers, have to pack themselves into single rooms?

The people will say to their slum lords: "If you don't give better accommodation and at lower rents, we shall go out to the People's Camp, where we will get roomy and comfortable houses for nothing."

This brings me again to that building question upon which I have already touched slightly. The other day I met a man of considerable average intelligence and much practical knowledge of life, now farming in Ireland, but who had been a working man in many countries. He assured me that the long apprenticeships served by boys to their trades were not at all necessary. He took bricklaying as an instance. "Give me," he said, "an intelligent, willing lad of 13 or 14, and I'll undertake that after a fortnight, he will be laying brick as a bricklayer."

I should be sorry to advise anything which might draw down wages in any trade or occupation. But the Trek and the consequent numerous creative activities going forward will not be in competition with any occupation, but rather [they will] assist all occupations by the withdrawal of labour from the labour market and [by the] provision of an alternative mode of life to those who, having no other resource, are compelled to sell their labour and to sell it, therefore, at a low price.

I imagine your first settlement as a tented Camp, but a tented Camp, which is rapidly becoming a well-built City with hundreds of enthusiastic young masons, bricklayers, and carpenters at work there busy as bees. You will want many homes for your young married people and your young people who want to be married.

In everything do the exact opposite of Civilisation and you won't go wrong. Now Civilisation bans marriage. It says to young people, "Don't marry; if you do I will hunt you." And you know the awful consequences[90] which arise from that crime, from the millions upon millions of young people whom our devilish Civilisation compels to be celibates.

You will in every way encourage young people to marry, and to that end make an ample provision of houses and homes.

When your builder boys are ready to work, perhaps your own brick kilns will be ready to supply them with bricks. If not, they can be got from the brick kilns of the interior. I have often seen barges laden with bricks coming down along the two great canals traversing the Country.

You might aim at starting your own potteries also, getting your earths, perhaps, in the first instance, from Cornwall, as even the famous Staffordshire potteries do to-day.

Aim in every direction at making yourselves, the things that you need. Even rude things made by yourselves will give far greater pleasure to the users than much finer things which are bought.

Buy the very least amount that you can, remembering that everything bought has been the subject of exploitation, of usury, and has been wrought by sweated labour. Buy as little as possible; sell nothing.

Please pardon me this use of the imperative mood. I only express myself so for the sake of brevity.

As I pondered over the tragedy presented by our vast modern cities, my thoughts, as they often do, came up again in an imaginative form. As it may be a help to you to understand I shall describe what I saw. Also, a story is easier to remember than bald reasonings.

A great warrior, having stormed and sacked a town, and massacred most of the inhabitants, drove the survivors into a single huge building, barred and bolted the iron door, and marched away to meet an advancing enemy. The great dungeon resembled the Black Hole of Calcutta in this, that it was provided with only a single window, strongly grated. Soon the prisoners, knowing that the air was being poisoned by their own exhalations, began to move towards that window with a motion which presently became a mad rush of the panic-stricken multitude craving air, only air; knowing that the alternative was death. Fear reigned in every heart, fear, the most cruel of the passions. Women, children, the old, the weak of every kind, many strong men, too, were flung down and trampled upon. A few powerful men, owing to the mere accident of their position, were able to lay hold upon the window stanchions. These they clutched and held on to with the tenacity of despair.

In this chamber of horrors and madness I saw a young man hurled violently against one of the walls. It was the western wall of the great dungeon which like the rest seemed to be built of solid granite. Recovering from that violent impact he stood a moment reflecting, some thought, some wild surmise suddenly taking possession of his mind. The rush of the multitude had left him a free space, and with it an opportunity of recovering his reason.[91]

He now clenched both his fists and pounded upon the granite wall. The resulting sounds I could not hear amid shrieking and wailing, the shoutings and the tramplings; but he heard them and knew their meaning. That west wall, which seemed to be of granite like the rest, was only painted wood.

He laid hold upon his nearest neighbour, roared in his ear, violently compelled him to approach that wall and to beat upon it as he had done. The two then dealt so with others and these again with others.

Soon, I saw a score or two of strong men, and scattered amongst them many women and girls, press and press again, with all their might and with one accord and impulse, against that western wall, which bent, and bent, and broke! The blessed air and the light of heaven streamed into and flooded the whole dungeon. There was a moment's silence after that continuous storm of shrieks and cries, followed by a joyous shout as the imprisoned multitude rushed forth, but as quickly returned, dragging out with them or carrying the dying and the dead, those whom but a moment since they had been trampling to death in the ruthlessness of their terror.

I need not explain my poor parable, least of all to you who know so well the lives led in great cities by the vast mass of the people there congested—the fury of competition for wages, salaries, jobs, berths, for some share, less or more, of that without which the people cannot live at all. Dublin, like every great modern city, is a vast prison, into which the Money-God has allured, drawn, driven you, and keeps you fast held in a state of murderous, fratricidal strife. But on one side, that which faces westward, looking towards the great prairies of Ireland, the wall that looks like solid granite is only painted lath.[92]

Burst it, you men and women of the Unions taking the lead, irresistible in your combined strength, escaping into God's pure air and light, into the plains, valleys, hillsides of Ireland, leading forth with you the poor, trampled, perishing people.

There, waiting for you with beckonings and invitation, are angels, none the less real because just now only visible to the eye of Faith. Plenty—plenty of all manner of good things—and health and strength and happiness and hope that knows no bounds, and leisure, and, above all, Freedom, the reality of that for the very shadow of which so many millions of brave men have immolated themselves, and mostly in vain.

Think of the countless lives lost since the beginning of history in the wild pursuit of the mere shadow or reflection of freedom. For you see now—you have England and American to teach you—that political freedom is not freedom at all, but a change of tyrants, and, generally, a change for the worse.

The Irish Worker, 5 April 1913, p. 1, cols. 1–2.

TO OUR LABOUR LEADERS.
(CONTINUED.)

Consider that wise and very socialistic little animal, the bee. Once at a country house a young girl told me that the bees had a language of their own, and that it was "Irish". When I laughed, she left the room, but soon came back, with a lit lantern in her hand—it was night—and bade me go with her. She led me out through the dark to her row of bee-hives, and stopping at one of them bade me stoop down and listen.

From within came a great continuous surge of sound, waves of sound rising and falling without intermission.

"Do you know what they are saying?" she asked.

"No," said I.

"They are saying—'Fang, fang,' that is leave, leave. They'll be swarming to-morrow."

And certainly that great Trek-song of the bees was not so very much unlike the sound of the Gaelic word Fang.[93]

When the bee population becomes excessive, when there is not honey enough for all, the bees, with a wisdom greater than ours and a fine spirit of adventure, hope and faith, conceive and accomplish a grand exodus or trek around their queen, led, one might almost think, by God himself; surely inspired, impelled, guided by a guardian spirit, deriving its wisdom from the infinite wisdom which made and upholds all things. They go out into the unknown, nothing doubting.

If the bees were mad enough they might imitate humanity; they might wage war upon each other for the honey. But they know that if they did the bee race would come to an end. They spare their fellow-citizens; they abandon, give up, all claim to the honey which they have themselves made. They trek, establish a new home, and in a few weeks that new home is bursting with honey, overflowing with a fresh and vigorous population, and preparing in its turn to be a metropolis, that is a mother city in its own right, and send forth swarms of its own.

Learned men say that but for man the bees would conquer the Globe, such is their wisdom, courage, patriotism; their determined Socialism and astonishing fecundity.

If—and God grant you the courage and the wisdom to do so—if you trek and establish a new Dublin in the Shire of Dublin, that new Dublin will soon fling out a third, and these three swarm again and again and again.

Don't aim low, don't aim at little and mean things. Aim first at the conquest and annexation of your own great County of Dublin. Dublin and Dublin Shire always went together in old times. The old Danish Kingdom of Dublin—sometimes, too, an Empire and governing Man and the Hebrides—included the whole County; County Wicklow also, if I don't mistake. The very name of the County is Danish.

When Henry II, as Lord of Ireland, Dominus de Hibernia, gave Dublin to the stout Norman Conquistador, Milo de Cogan,[94] he did not give him only a barren collection of houses and fortifications on Cork Hill. He joined the Shire to that great grant as "mensal land",[95] so that Milo's table might be well supplied, lacking nothing, and his hospitalities brilliant and worthy of a Prince.

Men of Dublin, won't you conquer back your own country, annexing Wicklow, too, for your sheep for the provision of your wool, and as a grand playground for your young people and a source of inspiration for your artists and poets, sowing it far and wide with your settlements and guest houses, where no bills will be presented and no shame-faced or insolent wardens stand around for tips?[96]

I am not asking you to do anything impossible. I should be sorry to trifle with a situation so grave, even so terrible and tragical, as that which challenges our attention in Dublin to-day; the children without food, without air, without light; the unemployment, the casual and intermittent unemployment; the disgracefully low standard of wages; the intolerable rents even for single rooms; the growing mental depression of the people, and the decline of their spirit in consequence. Dublin men are not now buoyed up as they used to be with the thought of "Ireland a Nation among the Nations of the Earth."[97] I remember when the bare thought of it made them feel as if they were treading on air.

No, I am not trifling. I see clearly that if you can rekindle, and in this direction, the slackening fires of their hope and faith, all that I have suggested and more, and a great deal more, is realizable, and even easy realizable, once that such a spirit takes possession of their minds and when the first exodus in that spirit is successfully accomplished. The first Camp, founded in the right spirit, erected upon a basis of the agricultural and manufacturing industrial activities and adequately equipped from the enormous collective financial resources of the people, that first Camp will rapidly breed a second, deriving its equipment mainly from the first.

If you ask me, "What is that right spirit?" I think I cannot do better than remind you of something within your own personal experiences. You have more than once taken part in a pleasant picnic in the County Wicklow, going in drags with music and singing, good nature in every heart and good humour on every face, and good cheer stowed away in your baskets. That is the right spirit—the holiday spirit. You remember how that day the young and strong helped the old and feeble over rough places, and the athletes carried little children in their arms; how volunteer lads and lassies sallied out to gather sticks for the fire and draw water for the kettles. Now, everyone did everything in his power to make the picnic a success. Perhaps you yourself fell in love that day; it is not unlikely. You remember the spirit of that picnic—everyone anxious to give, and no one anxious to get—and yet, in spite of that universal spirit of giving, no one was in want and everyone was happy. Everyone got and got abundantly. That is the spirit—the spirit of the holiday and the picnic—in which you must conduct that first great Trek and Exodus, the spirit in which you will pitch your first Camp in the great and bloodless war for the abolition of poverty and the recovery of your native land.

If you can achieve one victory like that, a victory, in the first instance, over yourselves, your own mean impulses and sordid, small personal ambitions, the ambition to get a "berth", or to live upon usury, or to drive a small business in sweating labour, don't you think that lands and monies and everything you require will keep flowing towards you?

I know they will. That is how the world is made. Go right and straight and bold, and all such material things recognise their lord and master, and of themselves answer his call and submit to his pleasure.

I could quote a great text here, but forbear. It begins, "Seek ye first."[98] The present social order is founded upon the verb to get; the new social order, now everywhere struggling to emerge, and which surely somewhere, if not here, will emerge and rapidly embrace the world, will be founded on the verb to Give.

Now, in spite of all indications to the contrary, it is more natural and more human to give than to get. Your picnic was a success because instinctively you recognised this truth.

So when I say to you, trust in voluntary activities, I am only asking you to trust in a grand perennial and even universal human instinct.

The Irish Worker, 19 April 1913, p. 1, col. 4.

THE CAMP.

A general summer camping-out of the working population of Dublin would be the greatest event in the history of Ireland up to date. It can only be accomplished through a successful appeal to the heart and soul of the people, because, without such an appeal, it would be impossible to raise the funds necessary for carrying through an undertaking of that magnitude. Of our population of 500,000, there are probably 50,000 who could hardly subscribe to the camping-out fund at all. Unless this 50,000 are helped by the 200,000 who are able to put in pennies, sixpences, shillings, and half-crowns, that project, the noblest and most promising that has come up in Ireland in my time, breaks down necessarily.

No one can be expected to take a serious interest in a movement which aims at encouraging people who can afford it to join with other people who can afford it and erect and maintain summer camps, each of the nature of a joint stock enterprise.

Some such camps, owned by spirited Dublin clerks and shop assistants I have often observed, and with great pleasure, scattered here and there in the county, and within easy reach of Dublin.

My heart goes out always to these brave young men and their camps; but the camping out of the working population of Dublin is a different thing altogether, and must be aimed towards upon absolutely different principles. Here it must be all for all, and all for each, and each for all, and the resulting camp must be of the nature, not of joint stock enterprises, but something of the nature of communes for the time being, sustained from a centre supplied with the necessary resources, each camp loyally supporting that centre and submissive to its authority.

Besides, an appeal to the people—a separate people— should be made to the soul and consciences of our private citizens who are well off, and to the employing classes generally. I should be glad to take a part in the preparation of this appeal.

The movement ought, in my opinion, to be kept quite separate and distinct from the war of Labour and Capital.

I suggest that Miss Larkin, who has much practical ability and practical experience, should take a sole command of the movement, providing herself, of course, with a committee of experts and general advisers.

But I would like to see one person in control and responsible for everything.

One person assisted by a council has always been that kind of government which has produced the best results.[99]

A Committee with divided responsibility has, I think, never proved successful.

STANDISH O'GRADY.

The Irish Worker, 26 April 1913, p. 1, cols. 1–2.

TO OUR LABOUR LEADERS.
(CONTINUED.)

When I bade you aim at the conquest and annexation of the two great Counties of Dublin and Wicklow, I meant every word I wrote. But I assumed that you had already planted out, in the County of Dublin, a permanent Camp or City of 10,000 people, drawn out from our capital, well equipped with land, labour-saving machineries; all the means, ways, and instruments of production, and loyally sustained by the men of Dublin, and with all the fire and dash of the Irish nature, employed, like war soldiers, in the creation of life and of every rational form of wealth. Establish such an agricultural and industrial centre of even 10,000 people out in our county, filled with the resistless, divine fire which always accompanies the undertaking of a great enterprise, and the subsequent conquest and annexation of the two counties will seem a small thing in your eyes and only a preparation for something greater.

They, the 10,000, so equipped and so sustained, and well aware that the eyes, not alone of Dublin, but of all Ireland, are fixed upon them, will produce—what? They will produce probably enough to support themselves. They will produce enough to support a hundred times their number, enough to support a million. Make your own calculations; I have made mine.

No one here yet realises what the productivity of labour means to-day in this miraculous age. When the 8-shared plough, petrol driven, is walking over these plains you will better understand. In every direction evidences and proofs of this new gigantic power of man over matter are accumulating.

To-day I met a commercial traveller travelling in paper. He told me that in his Lancashire mill they have a machine which rolls out a sheet of paper 10 yards wide and at the rate of 100 yards a minute. He said "300 feet". I made him repeat the words. Five men attend the machine.

Would not the SCRAPPED machinery of such a mill enable your people to supply paper for millions? But in all directions, and in the production of every form of wealth, I find the same tale repeated.

Put your people on to the creation of wealth, and wealth you will have; and through that wealth—not through money, observe, for you will sell nothing, letting the markets shift for themselves. Through this wealth you will be able to annex the counties, townland by townland; for you will have the reality, of which money is the uncertain token—that is, solid wealth. You will have, in overflowing abundance, all these good material things necessary for the maintenance and the promotion of life.

Let me illustrate what I mean by a definite instance.

Recently I interviewed a tenant farmer in the Co. Wicklow, who, I heard, wished to sell his holding. It consisted of twenty acres of arable land, not good, but arable, and a considerable hinterland of mountain attached, enough to maintain some forty sheep. It was on the southern slopes by Lugnaquilla. For the farm he asked £100, and would probably have accepted £70.

He was an old man and decrepit. His family consisted of a daughter, who was feeble-minded, and a fine little boy, his grandson, of eleven.

Now, of what use would £100 be to such a family? They would probably drift into Baltinglass or Rathdrum with their £100, which would soon melt away and leave them quite ruined.

I assume now that you, having established a well-equipped settlement in the county, fed, sustained, and furnished in that first or parent Camp in the Co. Dublin, make the following proposition to the poor old, worn-out man;—

"If you give us the land, we will supply you and your daughter, for life, with all the milk, butter, potatoes, vegetables, oatmeal, wheatmeal, cloth, linen, cotton, tobacco, or anything else that you may reasonably require. Keep your home where you were born and were married and saw good times. We shan't disturb you at all in the secure possession of your old home.

As for the little boy, give him to us. We will take good care of him—educate him, provide for his future, and every Sunday send him to see you and his aunt, as is right."

Also you might promise him a small money annuity.

Would not this be a friendly and good arrangement for both the high contracting parties?

Three human beings, fallen into great trouble, would be thus well and amply provided for, released absolutely from the fear of want and the terror of the workhouse, with almost no expense to you; and you will have acquired the fee-simple of some eighty acres of that noble and romantic county.

The maintenance of that little family would mean no loss to you. Are not your 10,000 out in the Co. Dublin producing enough to maintain the whole population of the two counties, and to maintain them as they were never maintained before?

I may add that the farmhouse here and the out-offices could not, in my poor opinion, be erected for less than £100. All this would, of course, ultimately fall into your possession. You would make that part of the bargain. The annual rent or Government annuity and the rates were a bagatelle.

When I interviewed this old man I was the guest of an adjoining tenant, a widow woman. She was over eighty years of age, and managed and worked the farm, about twelve acres, with a heathery hinterland for sheep, through one of her sons, who was about 55, a bachelor.

There were two grandchildren under twelve. This little family, too, had failed, and would have been quite ready for a similar arrangement.

Dr. MacDermott, for 40 years an Irish dispensary doctor, in his very clever book, "The Green Republic",[100] maintains that nine-tenths of the so-called farmers of Ireland are unable to do justice to their lands owing to some form of disability, age usually, chronic sickness, feebleness of mind, drink, or sheer indolence.

Remembering this, I made close inquiries, and found that a very large proportion of the farmer families in this neighbourhood were in a condition of insolvency or approaching it.

When you move into that county, issuing your cheery summons and making your cheery proposals, "maintenance, a good maintenance for all and no one to be disturbed out of his home", you will have to send out there a very able administrator and a great supply of recruits to your branch camp, so much land will fall into your possession even from the start.

I have personally known several large mountain farms there sold for about £50. What are £50 to a family leaving their old homes, people generally incapable of earning a living, and going on to face the wide world with that sorry sum?

And I believe a similar state of things prevails too, if not so acutely, in the rich plains. The grazier people are failing. Their position is anomalous and absurd. They don't work. They keep the land in a state of nature. They do little more than just remain alive. Most of them will be only too glad to exchange their lands for that ample, generous, and splendid maintenance with which you will be able to supply them. Your advent, the establishment of your branch camp in any district will be like the coming of the Jubilee Year to the ancient Israelites.

For you are not capitalistic land-grabbers out on the prowl. You are friendly and generous, and can give twice and thrice as much as those poor people can ever make out of the land. Then you are always in a position to take care of their children, a great inducement to the old people.

You understand generally the plan of campaign which I am outlining. Its certain success depends upon the success of that central fixed camp of 10,000, representing the first exodus from Dublin.

For the lands of that first camp you will have to pay in cash down, but very soon the ownership of the surrounding lands will gravitate towards you.

Now, between you and the establishment of such an agricultural and industrial centre, with magazines and store chambers overflowing with every kind of wealth, there intervenes no material obstacle, none whatever.

I thank you, leaders of Irish labour, for permitting me to say my say in your paper. It was the more gracious, for I know well that you, like the labour leaders the world over, have your thoughts fixed upon an altogether different plan of campaign.

The Irish Worker, 3 May 1913, p. 1, cols. 1–2.

A POSTSCRIPT.

It will be objected that, though the rents and rates of a few score of holdings may be manageable enough, yet, when you take up great districts of these counties, the pecuniary liabilities will be so considerable that you will have to commercialise your great enterprise, to study the profitable, and aim at markets and money, like any vulgar joint stock company or co-operative society.

That, of course, would be the complete and shameful ending of the Trek as a revolutionary movement. You will remember that it was as the first step in a bloodless and beneficent social revolution that I brought before your minds the thought of an Exodus from Dublin and the foundation in the country of a centre of activity devoted only to the creation of wealth, and not to the exploitation of that wealth when produced.

Personally I am convinced that you will never lack for money if you conduct such an Exodus and in such a spirit, bringing out first the weak, infants and their caretakers, children, old people, the incapable; the unemployed and the "unemployables", with enough of strong, wise men and women to guide them, to teach and discipline. That is absolutely the law of the situation—the weak first. If you don't do this, if you aim in any other way, be it as promising and plausible as it may, at rending the net which Capitalism has woven around you, you will be defeated. Regard Dublin as a sinking ship— it is that—and yourselves as the crew, and act as brave men act in such a crisis, when strength stands aside and sees weakness fill the boats.

So, a blessing will follow you, as surely as I write these words; and the succeeding thousands of the strong and capable will go forward from strength to strength, and from victory to victory, assistants and assistances of a hundred kinds coming to your aid, inevitably. You will never lack money, or have to exert yourselves to get it, only in the first rough united stages of the movement. You know the story of the saints of old, how they trekked into the desert, turning their backs upon a world then dominated by Cain, as ours is by a viler lord, and now after a few years, though they went out empty, our island was filled with their wealthy and powerful religious foundations. Human nature is so made that it will pour forth its best, and lavishly, for the sustainment of any bold, generous, and magnanimous enterprise. This is as true as any axiom in political economy, or as any maxim frequent in the mouths of the worldly wise. Save in the beginning you will never lack for money.

I have asked you to imagine your wealth creating centres founded, well equipped, and already humming with a hundred different kinds of glad activity, and not industrial only but artistic and intellectual also. I have shown you how, without money, but through the teeming, varied wealth there created, you might buy out the poor cot-tenants of Wicklow, and the sluggish and failing grazier people of this county.

I recur now to that apparent difficulty as to the rents and rates of those districts which I imagine you as have got into your ownership and under your control. When you get so far, attaining to such a point as this, you will neither want money, nor will money be wanted from you. Money, as we know it, will then, and as a consequence of your action, have lost utterly its present terrible significance in our affairs.

But, as I cannot expect you, as yet, to see eye to eye with me in this matter, I shall now assume that the present dominance of money in our affairs, remain around us in its full strength, and that you experience a check by not being able to produce it in sufficient quantities to pay the rents and rates by the land which is yours.

Now, I perceive several ways by which men who possess great material wealth, resources, and a great power of wealth-production like you can supply themselves with necessary moneys without, like a dog to his vomit, returning to the unclean ways of commercialism, without rushing into the world's markets, and, so, ruining a movement which was started in order to enable you to escape from commercialism and from a vile subjection to the world's vile god.

Here is but a single instance of the many modes by which you might make money for necessary public purposes, and plenty of it, without rushing to markets and sending back to Dublin slums the thousands and tens of thousands whom you led into the country with the promise of Freedom.

Recently two young friends of mine bought an upland farm in Wicklow; four acres arable; about forty waste and heather, but containing a good turf bog. Rent and rates less than £2 a year. The situation beautiful; trout streams and trout lakes hard by.

In this neighbourhood a resident erected and furnished some years ago a plain bungalow for which she gets £8 a month during three months in summer and autumn. It has never been unlet. The building equipment, and furnishing cost her about £200.

I now assume that you, having bought that holding, and having a branch Camp planted in this neighbourhood, have erected there a bungalow as good as that which brings the lady £24 per annum. This you can do without the expenditure of money through the glad labours of layers, carpenters, joiners, makers of furniture, domestic utensils, etc. You could then let it as well as the lady lets hers: for £24 a year.

This £24 represents twelve times the rent and rates of that holding, which were only £2. Then, as its area was 44 acres, you have in the rent of this summer tenant enough to pay the rents and rates of twelve times as much land of a similar character, or of 528 acres of the highlands of Wicklow.

Again, this tenant and his family will need food, fuel, and other conveniences, with which you can supply him from your Camp in an ample manner. Compressed turf as good as coal; potatoes, milk, butter, vegetables, eggs in plenty; oatmeal, wheatmeal; rabbits probably; trout; the boys will see after this; for your streams, as fast as they fall into your possession, the boys will take care to keep well stored with trout. (I have not touched the meat question in any of these papers.)

Now, a man of means who is willing to pay £24 for a three months' good time in the country will be ready enough to pay at least £1 a week for the good things that I have just enumerated. That is £13, for the three months, which, with his rent, will bring you £37. This is more than the rents and rates of eighteen holdings similar to that upon which you have planted that bungalow and which consisted of 44 acres, rough and smooth. Therefore, this one bungalow, and let on such terms will meet the rents and rates of nearly 8,000 acres of the highlands and of the highland arable ground of the county.

Now, if you have only forty of such residences, and let on those terms, they will bring in a revenue sufficient to pay the rates and rents of near 33,000 acres of those highland regions, the ownership of which will give you also the ownership of the mountains. Of course, the claim is absurd; but it is made and generally recognised. Owning the mountain, you will, of course, reafforest them. There is hardly a tree to-day in all the western half of Wicklow.

I am anxious to familiarise your minds with the thought that when your people own the instruments of production, and have become themselves the creators of wealth that is, of good and desirable material things—the necessity for the production of money, specie, must inevitably be reduced year by year, and even month by month.

I shall be expecting you, after a while, to be building your own ships for the exchange of your superfluities with foreign lands—ships soundly built, well rigged and well furnished, and manned by your own merry Irish lads. Everything is possible if only you go right.

The Irish Worker, 10 May 1913, p. 2, Col. 4.

THE CAMP.

DEAR MISS LARKIN.—Congratulations on the starting of the camp. Don't mind its smallness; the greatest things begin small. I have stood with a foot on either bank of the Liffey, and have spanned—the Nore in the hills of North Tipperary. It was amusing to hear the people there saying proudly about the little trickler, "Yes, that's the Nore!"

But, why apprehend that the summer residents will look sourly or disdainfully? Are they not all poor, hard-working business people, anxious to get a little sunshine and pure air for themselves and their children, just like your people in the camp? I would not entertain such a thought for a moment, or let such a thought get into the minds of your young people. Then, everyone in these unsatisfying times is interested in any innocent social experiment. I once visited the "Garden City" of Letchworth. There, one day, I saw a score or so of strange-looking men and women being personally conducted round by Mr. Ebenezer Howard,[101] the founder of the city. I learned that they were the representatives of as many societies scattered over France, the rumour of that rather poor English social experiment having already run through the Continent.

Then, I assume that there is nothing "class" in your brave venture, and that, in its expansions and enlargements, broken business people, all broken people, will be welcome in your Camps. Very well-off families are breaking down every day and falling into the gulf, needing a harbour of safety and a City of Refuge as well as others. When the seed you are sowing to-day spreads out boughs to the Sun and Air, when you fling your branch-camps into Wicklow, you may find me requiring a three-roomed bungalow for myself,[102] a free seat at your tables a free admission, when in a social mood, to all the fun and hilarity there reigning.

Only, keep in mind the idea of all, All; and don't limit things.

There was a nought too much in one of the figures of my "Postscript", 8,000 for 800, when I was dealing with rents and rates.

Here I may remark that I think buildings erected in promotion of your idea ought not to be liable to rates. They should come under the legislative provision which exempts the buildings of religious and charitable institutions. Don't give way on this point without a fight. Your movement seems to be both. Later, a great many thousands of pounds may be involved in this question.

Your proximity to the sea should enable you to supply plenty of fish to the Camp. A friend and myself once took more than 200 plaice, in a short afternoon, off the point of Howth. If you start boats and fishing let me know, and I shall help. The boys will go into that work with alacrity, and so solve a good part of the food problem. Perhaps, with an old fisherman to instruct, they might even manage nets and make great hauls of mackerel in the Autumn.

All kinds of interesting possibilities will disclose themselves once you have some land to provide a starting point. May I suggest the thought of a little paper, your own, printed by volunteer labour, without advertisements, published in the interests of the Camp and of the movement generally? There are good hand presses with which to make a start, purchasable still in Dublin. I know one that was offered for £7 10s. The paper should, I think, be made as bright and gay as possible, good-natured and good-humoured, and quite free from all the fierce passions raging in the outer world. I hope too that you will have an abundance of music and all kinds of innocent amusements. If so there will not be a spot of Irish earth like the Camp. Where else are we free from strife and the dominance of wolfish passions?

If you think these rapid notes and commentings would serve any good purpose you are at liberty to print.

Yours faithfully,
Standish O'Grady.

NOTES

1   It is hard to determine which strike O'Grady has specifically in mind as there were many disputes in the two years prior to this writing that led to both lockouts and strikes. He does question here the efficacy of Jim Larkin's tactics of using sympathy strikes when "tainted goods" were to be transported. In any event Larkin addressed O'Grady's concern in June 1913 when he succeeded in organizing many of the farm workers near Dublin. In August 1913 the union won a wage increase from the County Dublin Farmers' Association, but attempts to organize farm workers on a permanent basis generally failed. See Emmet Larkin, *James Larkin, Irish Labour Leader 1876–1947* (Cambridge, MA: MIT Press, 1965), pp. 89–97; 116–18; and 269.

2   Luke 18: 25. "For it is easier for a camel to go through a needle's eye, than for a rich man to enter into the kingdom of heaven."

3   A. R. Orage (1873–1934).

4   O'Grady's following definition of Syndicalism is generally accurate but does not distinguish it from other modes of Socialist activism. Syndicalism was distinguished by its focus on economic action rather than political action. Thus strict Syndicalists were uninterested in forming political Labour parties and often viewed them as ways of slowing down revolutionary progress.

5   The succeeding section in italics appeared in *The Irish Worker*, 12 Oct. 1912. Upon revision then, O'Grady breaks off the discussion of Syndicalism that he has introduced and moves on to discuss the practicalities of breaking away from the capitalist system. On p. 12 he returns to the published 12 Oct. 1912 column but cuts the several paragraph discussion of Syndicalism here restored.

6   Peter Kropotkin (1842–1921) was the leader of European anarchist communism for forty years. O'Grady acknowledges the influence of Kropotkin on his thinking on other occasions as well. *The Conquest of Bread* was published in 1906.

7 William Cowper (1731–1800), "Light Shining Out of Darkness".

8 Strikebreakers or "scabs".

9 O'Grady seems oblivious to the inaptitude of using a comparison from such genteel school life.

10 Zephaniah 1: 13.

11 O'Grady is making a case for drastic change, but he is trying to channel the unions into a non-violent course of action. O'Grady never seems to have seen that calling for action does not necessarily channel that action into his desired direction.

12 Matthew 16: 18: "And I say unto thee, That thou art Peter, and upon this rock I will build my church; and the gates of hell shall not prevail against it." Therefore "capital" equals hell.

13 The succeeding section in italics appeared in *The Irish Worker*, 23 Nov. 1912 but was cut in the revised version.

14 O'Grady obviously did not expect the space that he was given in the newspaper for the next six months.

15 O'Grady seems to have a sophisticated understanding of this word, which is too often merely translated as "repent". O'Grady—a classical scholar—captures the idea of a movement of mind that the original Greek implies—not some simple readjustment to an accepted code. Like Larkin, O'Grady believed that the people had to change their whole orientation to the world or they simply would hold the same values as the capitalists.

16 In the TS version O'Grady here cuts "sudden" from the published version. "Sudden" seems to be the most threatening word on the page— its cutting an index perhaps to his fear of imminent violence. The word was published in 1912; he must have become more wary after that time. This part of the work shows that he had a good sense of the pulse of revolutionary activity as well as its impracticality.

17 A belief being challenged or at least questioned by many of O'Grady's contemporaries—Thomas Hardy, for example.

18 The published version includes here the phrase, "and not by the wise and learned but by young working people".

19 O'Grady repeats the theme of a series of columns written under the title, "The Great Enchantment", in *The Peasant and Irish Ireland* in 1908. Lady Gregory had printed similar essays under the same title in *Ideals in Ireland* (1901). O'Grady's ideas about enchantment have a certain occult ring to them.

20 J. Pierpoint Morgan (1837–1913), American banker and industrialist. O'Grady obviously thinks the readership will be familiar with Morgan's photograph. Perhaps Morgan's activities in consolidating American railroads and making them profitable would have particular interest for his Transport Union readership.

21 Revised version cuts "worthless" here.

22　The reference here is inexact and the number of victims may not coincide with current estimates. At the dedication of the great Aztec pyramid temple in Tenochtitlán, 20,000 captives are now believed to have been killed.

23　A term Larkin also used. Its usage in this kind of context may derive ultimately from More's *Utopia*. See also note 51.

24　The published version includes the following sentences: "But you would 'make a good use of your good fortune.' Yes, I know. Every Dives thinks the same, and, thinking so, he keeps adding to his millions in that simple belief."

25　At the Battle of Omdurman (2 September 1898), Lord Kitchener led a superior Anglo-Egyptian force against the Mahdist forces that had been in control of the Sudan since 1881. In the battle, the "Mahdist total losses were about 10,000 killed, 10,000 wounded, and 5,000 taken prisoner. The British had about 500 casualties." (*Encyclopaedia Britannica*). O'Grady is apparently referring to the slaughter implied in these statistics and using them as a caution against Irish insurrection against the British.

26　O'Grady echoes nineteenth-century romantic "racial" notions about the Celts. See, e.g., Matthew Arnold's *On the Study of Celtic Literatures*.

27　Matthew 10: 16."Behold, I send you forth as sheep in the midst of wolves; be ye therefore wise as serpents, and harmless as doves." O'Grady may be remembering (or intentionally forgetting) Newman's Sermon 20, "Wisdom and Innocence", from his *Sermons on Subjects of the Day*.

28　The words echo Yeats's poem, "The Cold Heaven", which was first published in 1912.

29　O'Grady is mapping out a plan for guerrilla warfare although his intent is to warn the workers of the probable result of direct confrontation with the British Army. He may also be attacking the syndicalist notion of "direct action" as opposed to the "indirect action" of constitutional socialist politics.

30　O'Grady has an amazingly deft understanding of the middle-class psyche that ultimately triumphed in Ireland.

31　Men who carried two large boards, one for the front and one for the back, that extended from the shoulders to the knees to picket.

32　A very ominous threat, subject to interpretation by the reader's own proclivity.

33　A remnant of O'Grady's class loyalty?

34　O'Grady accurately describes Wordsworth's opposition to the Poor Law Amendment Act of 1834 articulated in his *Postscript* to *Yarrow Revisited*.

35　O'Grady must have meant Wordsworth's "The Leech Gatherer" (1807). He published "We Are Seven" in 1798 and "Daffodils" in 1804.

36　Wordsworth was born in Cumberland and lived in Grasmere *c.*1800–13.

37　A very odd view of Paine's influence, perhaps, but O'Grady's text here restores "the proverbial inspiration of the Scriptures". O'Grady seems to see Scripture as quite revolutionary.

38 Ideas found in many of Carlyle's works, especially *Past and Present* and *Sartor Resartus*.

39 1 Timothy 6:10: "For the love of money is the root of all evil: which while some coveted after, they have erred from the faith, and pierced themselves through with many sorrows."

40 An echo of Shylock's famous speech in *The Merchant of Venice* 3.1.54: "If you prick us do we not bleed?" O'Grady thus associates the employers with Jews and, although he here is pleading for tolerance, he may be playing to the prejudices of his audience.

41 A key O'Grady idea: history is the representation of degeneration; prehistory is the time of virtue. He thus focused on an account of prehistoric Arcadia in his final utopian work, *Render to Caesar*.

42 O'Grady reflects his belief in the method of Barthold Georg Niebuhr (1776–1831). In writing his "bardic histories" (1878–80), he cites Niebuhr as his model. Niebuhr, the father of scientific history, believed the historian could recover the pre-history through the use of philology.

43 Psalms 133:1: "Behold, how good and how pleasant it is for brethren to dwell together in unity!"

44 Fighting words that O'Grady seems oblivious to.

45 In Part II of *Finn and His Companions* (1892), O'Grady recounts this story and introduces Arthur as the king.

46 O'Grady has no problem in advocating resistance even when outnumbered.

47 Revised version cuts the word "Socialistic" here.

48 An astute explanation of how money becomes a force in its own right.

49 The subject of two of O'Grady's books, *Red Hugh's Captivity* (1889) and *The Flight of the Eagle* (1897).

50 The edited text ends here. The next two paragraphs in italics end the published column for 30 Nov. 1912.

51 O'Grady seems to be aware how explosive this word is. In October 1913 Jim Larkin began to speak of a "Co-operative Commonwealth", and it became his slogan thereafter. Emmet Larkin credits AE with leading Larkin in this direction, but AE continually acknowledged his indebtedness to O'Grady. See Larkin, p. 167.

52 The preceding two paragraphs were cut from the revised version but appeared in *The Irish Worker* on 30 Nov. 1912.

53 Isaiah 52: 7. "How beautiful upon the mountains are the feet of him that bringeth good tidings, that publisheth peace; that bringeth good tidings of good, that publisheth salvation; that saith unto Zion, Thy God reigneth!"

54 The passage closely resembles a speech by Oiseen in chap. XII of O'Grady's *History of Ireland*, vol. I, 1878.

55 Genesis 27: 27. "And he came near, and kissed him: and he smelled the smell of his raiment, and blessed him, and said, See, the smell of my son is as the smell of a field which the Lord hath blessed."

56 A not-so-oblique attack on Catholic devotions to saints.

57 James Anthony Froude (1818–94), *The English in Ireland in the Eighteenth Century.* (1874; rpt. 1901).

58 History, therefore, distorts—a position consistent with O'Grady's preference for pre-history.

59 Carlyle's concept of history particularly as expressed in *On Heroes, Hero-Worship, and the Heroic in History* (1840).

60 Apparent licence for revolution.

61 It is puzzling that O'Grady here closely follows the language of Article 31 of the 39 Articles of the Church of England: "Of the one oblation of Christ finished upon the Cross: The offering of Christ once made is the perfect redemption, propitiation, and satisfaction for all the sins of the whole world, both original and actual, and there is none other satisfaction for sin but that alone. Wherefore the sacrifices of Masses, in the which it was commonly said that the priests did offer Christ for the quick and the dead to have remission of pain or guilt, were *blasphemous fables and dangerous deceits.*" It is indeed strange that O'Grady would use the Christmas issue to introduce sectarian language into an essay with a largely Catholic audience. Larkin, for example, always regarded himself as a Catholic.

62 Electoral successes by the Irish Labour Party.

63 Anarchist impatience with the machinery of constitutional democracy.

64 Talk of issuing a proclamation seems like unwitting inspiration for the declaration of the Irish Republic in 1916.

65 James William Petavel (1870–?) published *The Coming Triumph of Christian Civilisation* in 1911. It argues against State Socialism and in favour of small "production-for-use" co-operative communities. Like O'Grady, Petavel makes use of the language of the gospels to promote his program.

66 O'Grady thus inverts the idea that North America received the great benefits of Christianity and identifies capitalism with the devil.

67 A close rendering of Deuteronomy 23:19.

68 A type of battleship armed with heavy calibre guns mounted in turrets. A British battleship, the first of this type, was launched in 1906 and named *Dreadnought.* O'Grady seems to be referring to a recent Canadian government expenditure on battleships of this kind.

69 O'Grady clearly hopes for such a peaceful reconciliation between the current workers and the gentry of Ireland.

70 "Shellback" is the pseudonym of a frequent contributor to *The Irish Worker.* "Shellback" commented favourably several times on the suggestions made by O'Grady. A "shellback" is a sailor who has crossed the equator.

71 Delia Larkin, Jim Larkin's sister. She was often in charge of social and cultural projects of the union.

72 A phrasing suggestive of Evangelical religious worship.

73 The meaning of Sinn Féin.

74   An apparently odd idea of what will make for success.

75   Tom Wibberley, a professor at Queen's University, Belfast, published several books on farming, including *Continuous Cropping and Tillage Dairy Farming for Small Farmers* in 1915. It seems likely he is the person to whom O'Grady is referring.

76   A common idea in his "Great Enchantment" articles.

77   1 Corinthians 1: 27: "But God hath chosen the foolish things of the world to confound the wise; and God hath chosen the weak things of the world to confound the things which are mighty." O'Grady has revised St. Paul perhaps not so unwittingly as he may be equating the "wise" with the powerful—as the "world" so often does.

78   Proverbs 11: 24. "There is that scattereth, and yet increaseth; and there is that withholdeth more than is meet, but it tendeth to poverty."

79   A Romantic ideal, espoused by Maud Gonne as well as O'Grady.

80   O'Grady regards sports as having replaced religion as the "opium of the people".

81   Bradford was the site of a woollen mill that revolutionized the weaving of wool into cloth during the Industrial Revolution. Prior to 1914 increased productivity demands by management caused labour unrest at Bradford—a fact probably well known by O'Grady's trade union audience.

82   The treadmill that is the market economy.

83   O'Grady's naïveté is evident here: the image conjured up for labour leaders would surely evoke an association between blacklegs and these children.

84   An eerie foreshadowing, perhaps, of the uses of psychiatry in the Soviet Union. O'Grady sets up the possibility for seeing people who are unhappy with his Trek paradise as mentally disturbed.

85   O'Grady never gives up hope that the Captains of Industry will act benevolently, if given the chance.

86   A seven-day harvest festival.

87   O'Grady's reference is garbled, and he corrects it the following week. See p. 90. He means to cite Deuteronomy 23: 12–14, which enjoins in part: "Thou shalt have a place without the camp . . . when thou wilt ease thyself abroad, thou shalt . . . cover that which cometh from thee".

88   A kind of mud oven used by British troops in the field.

89   In Greek mythology, the river glows with fire but does not burn.

90   An apparent reference to the appalling number of prostitutes and pimps in Dublin at the time.

91   O'Grady, like Joyce, locates Irish creative escape from Dublin in going west, and going west is more a matter of mental, than physical, change. A favourite O'Grady idea, the Great Enchantment, argues that the imprisoning nature of society is self-maintained—an intriguing anticipation of Foucault perhaps.

92   Compare the ending of Joyce's "The Dead". The Trek then resembles the journey westward.

93   A form of the verb "to wander or stray".

94   Strongbow's second in command (d. *c.*1183).

95   The land that comes with the office of chief in Brehon Law.

96   O'Grady seems to be remembering a scene from vol. 1 of his *History of Ireland* in which Coelshanig demands gratuities from Laeg, Cuculain's charioteer, in advance of providing hospitality. A similar scene may be found in *The Masque of Finn*.

97   Perhaps a reference to the long-delayed Home Rule Bill.

98   Matthew 6: 33. "But seek ye first the kingdom of God, and his righteousness; and all these things shall be handed unto you."

99   O'Grady never wandered too far from Carlyle's idea of the Great Man although a Great Woman would apparently be quite all right, too.

100   William Robert MacDermott (1838–1918), [pseud. A. P. A. O'Gara], *The Green Republic: A Visit to South Tyrone* (London: T. Fisher Unwin 1902).

101   Ebenezer Howard (1850–1928) was influenced by Frederick Law Olmstead in America, but also Ruskin, Shaw, and Morris among others in England. He led the movement to set up a city that would include gardens and other ecologically progressive urban spaces. Letchworth was begun in 1904 in England and became a model for urban planning elsewhere.

102   O'Grady may not have been just speaking idly here. He feared for the Anglo-Irish, perhaps even himself.